ENCYCLOPAEDIA OF
|Lures|

ENCYCLOPAEDIA OF
Lures

Chris and Sue Harris

The Crowood Press

First published in 1993 by
The Crowood Press Ltd
Ramsbury, Marlborough
Wiltshire SN8 2HR

British Library Cataloguing-in-Publication Data

A catalogue record for this book is available from the British Library.

ISBN 1 85223 737 6

Acknowledgements

We would like to thank all those people – friends, customers and lure
manufacturers, too numerous to mention – who have been so generous with
their help in the writing of this book.

Typeset by Footnote Graphics, Warminster, Wilts.
Printed and bound in Great Britain by
BPCC Hazell Books Ltd
Member of BPCC Ltd

CONTENTS

INTRODUCTION

What This Book Is

The *Encyclopaedia of Lures* gives a full description of nearly 300 lures. They have been chosen because they are a cross-section of lures which British anglers can obtain relatively easily; either in local tackle shops, from specialist tackle shops or by mail order (details of suppliers can be found in Appendix A). Some of the lures we've included will take a bit of hunting down, and some, by the time you read this book, will have gone out of production. Inevitably, there will be some favourites missed out, but a fully comprehensive guide to every existing lure would run into several volumes!

The book gives a brief outline of each lure, what it does and how it can be used. Each main entry is accompanied by an illustration. There are also alternatives suggested for some lures which do a similar job and which you might like to try.

The book will help the novice lure angler identify which lures do what – untangling the maze of strange names and descriptions which seem designed to baffle.

What This Book Is Not

This book is *not* an instruction manual on how to fish with lures. There are lots of good books on the subject, and some of these are listed in Appendix B. We would encourage every beginner lure angler to read some or all of these books; it will greatly add to his or her enjoyment of lure fishing.

The weekly and monthly angling publications are a great source of information. Contributors to look out for include Charlie Bettell, Mick Brown, Steve Burke, Gord Burton, Dave Cooling, James Holgate, Chris Leibbrandt, John Milford, Ian Parsons, Barrie Rickards, John Roberts, Des Taylor, Mike Thrussell and John Worzencraft, to name but a few.

As we write, the Lure Anglers' Society of Great Britain has just been launched, and this looks like a worthwhile society to join. Details of this, and other organizations of interest to lure anglers, are included in Appendix C.

Lure Fishing in the UK Today

Lure fishing spans coarse, game and sea fishing, from tiny fly spoons for sea trout and perch through deep diving plugs for pike, right up to the huge surface lures for the massive marlin and sailfish of the world's deep oceans.

In the US, lure fishing, strongly supported as the country's main method of sport fishing, has developed into a highly complex and very popular sport. In the UK, lure fishing has had its supporters and advocates, but has never really achieved the popularity it enjoys in the States or in continental Europe.

Spinning has for many years been the 'alternative' pike fishing method when live or dead bait fails. For many people, it meant a few chucks out with a rusty-hooked spinner, more in hope than expectation, then back to the baits. Small wonder then, that spinning got the reputation of being unproductive.

A few years back, however, Gareth Edwards caught a British Record pike on a Mepps Aglia spinner. Many scoffed and muttered, 'Fluke!'. Then in September 1992, along came Roy Lewis, who from the same water, Llandegfed, caught the current British Record pike (46lb 13oz) on a completely different lure, an old wooden Creek Chub Pikie minnow.

Thus Britain's largest and second largest officially recognized pike were both caught on lures – not to mention the many other fine fish caught on lures from this water and others like it. With clear evidence that big pike *do* take lures, and many waters adopting a lures-only policy, the profile of lure fishing started to be raised, as did its status, particularly as a piking technique.

Thanks to the fanatical enthusiasm of a relatively small number of people, lure fishing has become recognized increasingly for what it is; an exciting and challenging method of fishing, more than equal in excitement and effectiveness to other methods of catching predatory species. One considerable attraction is that, unlike most forms of fishing, lure fishing doesn't need a whole day's activity. Indeed, some of the best lure fishing can be had in a couple of hours after dawn or at dusk, wandering along the river bank or beside your favourite lake with rod and reel, a landing net and a small box of lures. For today's busy people, the need for short periods of leisure is increasing, and lure fishing fits in well.

So, if you'd like to come out from behind the Optonics and take a walk along the bank, or if you're just starting fishing for pike and fancy lure fishing, read on . . .

CHAPTER ONE
BEGINNING IN LURE FISHING

So you've tried the odd bit of lure fishing, have decided it's for you, and want to get into it more seriously, or perhaps you're just starting out from absolute scratch. Where do you begin?

Basic Equipment

Before you rush out and buy all those tempting lures, make sure you've got the essential tackle for lure fishing – in particular, for pike.

● A decent **landing net**, not the net you land 8oz roach with, but a large rimmed (30in minimum), deep net (36in or thereabouts). A round one is ideal but a collapsible triangular net is fine. Remember, you might catch a very large fish, in which case you want to be able to land it safely and without nearly bending it in half in the net.

● If you're going to be fishing from a hard bank or from a boat, you should have an **unhooking mat,** or at least something soft on which to lay your fish whilst unhooking it. If they thrash fish can bruise very easily, damage their scales and lose protective slime on rough ground. There is no need to buy an expensive mat at first (though they are excellent); you can improvise with, for example, a thick piece of foam rubber with a taped-on plastic bin liner cover.

● Thin-nosed **pliers, artery forceps** and **side cutters** for hook removal. Pliers are good where you need leverage. Artery forceps are slimmer and easier to use on small fish. Side cutters are needed for occasional emergencies, particularly with very small fish where a hook has penetrated awkwardly and must be cut away. Personally, we find the ridges that enable artery forceps to be gripped closed are a nuisance, and file them off. Another good tip is to shorten the nose of the forceps, giving much better leverage.

● **Wire traces** (essential for pike and zander, or for waters where they may be present).

● You can use any **rod** and **reel** for starters – an old feeder rod or carp rod is ideal – stiff rather than soft.

● **Line** should be matched to the size of fish you're aiming for (a minimum of 12lb for pike), and should be as limp as you can find. Look for American brands, such as Silver Thread AN40, which tend to be much less stiff than European brands.

● You'll need a **box** for your lures, and eventually you may want to invest in one of the purpose-made American ones. In the meantime, an old tool box is just fine.

These are only the basics; fuller coverage of lure fishing tackle falls outside the scope of this book. Do read up on the subject and make sure that when you catch your first fish on a lure, you are capable of handling it properly. Pike in particular are very delicate creatures, despite their teeth and ferocious reputation. They will not survive bad handling.

Unhooking a Pike

We make no apologies for focusing on pike, as they are the main focus of much lure angling, and besides, they are our own favourite fish. A lot has been said and written about care of pike, and the best way to learn is to go fishing with an experienced pike angler. However, most people have to learn on their own by experience, so here is a brief step-by-step guide.

1. Remove the pike from the landing net – watch out at all times for gill flaring which means the pike is about to thrash – beware of trebles catching in the net.

2. Lay the pike down on its back on an unhooking mat or something soft. Position this as near to the water as possible – try not to carry the fish around.

3. If the fish is large, kneel gently astride the pike; this will stop it thrashing. (We almost always wear waterproof overtrousers which do not remove too much slime.)

4. Insert a finger (left hand if right handed and *vice versa* – thumb on the outside) into the centre of the gill covers and slide up towards the front of the mouth. Your fingers will curl around the lower jaw. *The pike will not bite you.*

5. Hold fairly tightly, keeping a watch for the gill flaring warning, and lift the weight of the pike's head off the mat. His (or her) mouth will automatically open. If it doesn't, lift a little more of the shoulders off the ground.

6. The hooks should be clearly visible in the side of the mouth and can be removed with long-handled forceps or pliers. The good news is that when lure fishing, you will rarely have a deep-hooked fish. Indeed, the vast majority of fish are hooked in the side of the jaw, called the scissor, and many fish can be lifted with

the finger-under-the-gill-cover technique directly out of water, unhooked in a second and put straight back. But just in case things aren't so straightforward, here's the rest of the technique for unhooking pike.

7. If the hooks are out of sight (extremely rare when lure fishing but possible if the bait is sucked in completely), put firm pressure on the trace until the hooks come into view. Then unhook as before. If the hooks are difficult to remove, snip off the bend with side-cutters. The pike's gullet is like a sock and can be turned almost inside out without damaging the fish. When unhooked, push the gullet gently back into position with your forceps.

8. When dealing with a deeply hooked fish, *speed* is more critical than surgical accuracy. Get those hooks out and the pike back into the water as soon as possible, *especially during the summer*. Holes and small tears in the pike's gullet will quickly mend.

9. Ease the pike back into the water gently. If it was a long fight, you may have to hold the fish upright in the water, holding it until it's ready to go – it'll let you know when.

Hooks – Barbed or Unbarbed?

When deadbaiting (or livebaiting), we believe semi-barbless hooks are essential. They are far easier to remove from your fish, your net and, in the worst case, your hand! Barbless hooks are not essential for lure fishing: the fish are rarely hooked in a difficult position and the hooks come out easily. However, we still remove the barbs from most of our lures.

Safety First

If you're piking, you will probably want to wear gloves for unhooking. Usually people recommend gardening gloves, but these are often very heavy and thick, meaning that you lose all sensitivity when handling the fish, which has to be a bad thing for the pike. Until recently (preferring to damage ourselves than a fish), we've usually handled pike bare handed, except for a leather finger stall on the middle finger of the left hand, as protection from scratches from the gill rakers. This was simply because we couldn't find gloves we were happy with. We've now come across a brand in our local DIY store, which are made of a soft chamois-type leather. They are reasonably cheap, come in mens' and ladies' sizes (the ladies' size is ideal for youngsters or those with small hands), combine protection with softness and sensitivity, and fit a lot better than the average pair of cardboard boxing gloves we've tried in the past. They also dry out quickly and keep your hands warm in winter.

If you're around lures and fish, sooner or later there's going to be blood – yours. We always take with us a pack of absorbent dressings, and a roll of micropore tape for patching ourselves up. Don't worry about cleaning up wounds there and then; antibiotics will cope with any infection which might come along, and river water could do more harm than good. Try to keep any cuts dry, and bear in mind the possibility of Weils Disease, should you get the symptoms of flu over the following days. A spot of quick first aid allows you to go on fishing instead of being forced to pack up and go home – but do be sensible.

Starting your Lure Collection

So, how do you go about building a lure collection from scratch? First, don't go out and buy dozens of exotic and flashy looking plugs, spinners and spoons, tempting though that may be. Your most important asset when fishing is confidence. You must believe you're going to catch a fish. When starting out, the

first few successes are important, and the sooner they come the better. This way you will quickly come to realize that perch, pike, chub, trout, sea trout, zander, salmon and nearly all sea species *will* take that strange-looking piece of plastic, wood or metal.

So how do you go about building this confidence? The answer is, *keep it simple*. Start out with a small selection of spinners and spoons (if you aren't confident about the differences, they're explained later). Aim to catch a few fish from your favourite water first, and *then* start experimenting. The opportunities for experimentation are virtually endless; you'll find long and short range lures, spinners, wobblers, floaters, chuggers, shallow divers, deep divers, sinkers, vibrators and many more, all of which will catch fish on their day.

When building your lure collection, you'll want to start trying all the various types of lure, but always bear in mind the kinds of waters you mainly fish. If it's a large, deep, concrete-bowl-type reservoir, then you'll be focusing on deep divers, vibrators and sinkers. On the other hand, if you generally fish a small, weedy lake, you'll probably want to concentrate on shallow divers and surface lures. Similarly, a fast, deep river calls for sinkers and spinners, and so on.

When choosing lures, it pays to buy good quality, of course. However, there is an argument for buying cheap lures in one particular situation; that is, when you're going to fish a very snaggy or rocky swim and you are fairly certain that you're going to lose a lot of lures. You can sacrifice some of your cheapies whilst checking out the swim, and if you start to catch, you then have the option of using your better-quality favourites in the hope of picking up a good fish.

As most of us manage to fish a variety of waters, you'll get a chance to use a wide range of lures over time, but at the start, stick to the ones which you will use most often – those which suit your favourite water.

Do It Yourself

One of the beauties of lure angling is that you don't have to spend large amounts of money starting up. Try making a few lures of your own. A simple spoon is easy to make. Take an ordinary household spoon, cut off the handle, drill a hole in each end, one for the hook and one for the lure attachment. Paint to suit your taste and imagination, or just leave plain. Add a tag of red wool to the hook, and you're in business. Similarly, wooden plugs can be carved from pine, balsa or other soft wood (try broom handles), and kits for assembling your own spinners and spinnerbaits are also available. It's worth a try, even if you're not a DIY enthusiast, for the pleasure of catching a fish on a home-made lure.

Where to Buy

Where can you go to buy your lures? There are two main sources, shops and mail order companies, and as you would expect, both have their advantages and disadvantages.

Shops

If you have a local tackle shop with a good selection of lures, then this should probably be your first port of call. It's probable that one or more of the people behind the counter is an enthusiast; find out who it is and pick his or her brains. You'll probably get good information on the lures which are suitable for your local waters and for the species you are targeting. You can examine and compare the lures you find there, and choose what takes your fancy. In many ways it's the ideal way to buy.

The problem is that many tackle shops don't carry a good range of lures. This is partly due to the fact that many tackle-shop proprietors are not lure anglers, and partly due to the sheer economic difficulty of carrying a good stock of lures which may only be of interest to a small percentage of customers. Sad to say as well, some shops don't like to carry lures because they are so vulnerable to shoplifting.

Mail Order

For many years keen lure anglers bought their lures from the American mail order companies. Lure fishing was developed commercially in the US, and over there, it is very big business indeed. Several American mail order houses, such as Bass Pro and Cabelas, will ship to the UK. It's also possible to buy lures by mail from UK specialists, and their catalogues, though on a smaller scale, are starting to rival those of the Americans for lures.

The American companies offer a fantastic range of lures, and at first sight prices look cheap. However, you will be charged UK VAT and Customs and Excise Duty (currently 24 per cent in total) on delivery, not forgetting the high shipping costs. Also to be added in is the cost of buying a bank draft or international money order if you don't use a credit card. And of course, there will be a wait until you get the goods. On the other hand, it's definitely worth considering if you really can't find what you want in the UK.

UK mail order companies are becoming a good source of lures, and some very reputable companies involved will provide good customer service and advice, as well as a good range of products. There is also an ever-changing fringe of companies which are run by their enthusiast owners more or less as a hobby, and which can sometimes offer bargain prices. You'll find these companies advertised in the specialist magazines. (These companies do tend to come and go, so be sure you know who you're dealing with before sending off your money!)

What to Look for When Buying Lures

The choice of where to buy is up to you, but there are a few simple guidelines to follow when choosing lures.

1. Cheap unbranded imitations can be very useful, especially if you are building your collection on a low budget, or if you are fishing very snaggy swims and don't want to see your favourite lures sacrificed to underwater obstructions. However, do check for quality – cheap lures have a bad habit of falling apart in your hands or, worse still, in a fish's mouth. However, cheap doesn't have to mean nasty, and there are plenty of budget lures available if you shop around. Try to buy only named lures from a known manufacturer.

2. Look at all lures closely, even those bearing brand names, to ensure that the fittings are good and strong, vanes are fitted evenly and hook mounts are secure.

3. Don't get carried away by attractive names. It's no good buying a Whopper Stopper Magnum Hellbender if you plan to fish a four-foot deep drain over three feet of weed. Match the lures you buy to the waters you plan to fish.

Colour

One of the most debated subjects amongst lure anglers is colour – which colours work best and why?

We do not know for sure whether fish can distinguish colour. Until fish learn to talk to us (and us to them), we will never establish with certainty whether, and why, they prefer gold to silver, or red to blue. In the meantime, we have to work on a combination of experience, probability and common sense. One thing we do know for sure is that there *are* days when the right lure in the wrong colour won't catch. Equally, there are those all too rare days when fish will take almost anything.

The only answer is to experiment on your local waters, and try to find out which colours work best under what conditions. Keeping a lure diary helps, noting down failures as well as successes.

Generally speaking, however (and this is where commonsense comes in), patterns such as perch, shining silver and shining gold are likely to work because they look like natural prey. In clear water, try to imitate the food on which your target species is likely to be feeding. In coloured water, go for fluorescents, flashing metallics and lures which emit strong sound signals. Remember from which direction the fish will be looking at the lure – behind, sideways, below – and choose your lure accordingly. Choose natural-coloured lures in clear water; bright ones in coloured water. There are no hard and fast rules, and plenty of mysteries. Why is a white lure with a red head so effective? Or is it a self-fulfilling prophecy: they're used a lot, so they'll catch a lot?

Just to confuse matters still further, American lure manufacturers have a colour language all of their own. Common names you may come across are listed below. (Many of them are the names of American fish.)

● **Shiner** A roach-like colour, generally silver.

● **Shad** A dull greyish white with a greenish back, often with a scale finish.

● **Pumpkinseed** An orange/gold colour with small dark speckles.

● **Fire Tiger** A very vibrant combination of fluorescent green, orange and yellow.

● **Coach Dog** A spotty, dalmatian dog pattern, often black on white, though other combinations occur.

● **Crawdad** A natural crayfish print, usually orange/brown.

13

- **Sunfish** A fish print, gold and orange colours.

- **Bass** Similar in colour to a gudgeon.

- **Frog** Green and yellow spots on a light green body is the most common interpretation, but several other frog themes exist.

- **Chartreuse** (Pronounced shar-trurs, to rhyme with furs.) A bright limey yellow.

- **G-Finish** A deeply iridescent finish.

Where to Go First

You're ready to go out now, so take yourself off to a smallish water and run your lure as slowly as possible past reed beds, obstructions, along the face of inlets and bays, in fact, anywhere a predator might be lurking in wait for a meal. Spring, summer and autumn are the best times to begin, but lures will catch in winter too.

If you're lucky enough to be within reach of the sea and a rocky shoreline or a steeply shelving beach, try casting a spinner off the rocks during the spring and summer months. Spinners, spoons and plugs of all types will take mackerel, garfish, bass and indeed most other species of salt-water fish. Baited spoons, particularly in estuaries, are a deadly way of attracting flounders and plaice.

Lure Maintenance

Lures in use need to be looked after. The hooks are the obvious weak point. Be suspicious of your hooks right from the moment you open the box your lure first came in. If in doubt, change the hooks to a reputable brand. Partridge, VMC, Mustad and other manufacturers all produce excellent quality hooks. Replace over-large or thick hooks, but when you do so, check that your new hooks aren't un-

balancing the lure's action. Lead wire wound around the shank of the new hook is useful for rebalancing.

Critically important is keeping hooks sharp. Lure hooks are subject to a lot of wear and tear, so keep a sharpening stone in your box and use it! Try not to put wet lures back in your box, as this will result in rust. A packet of silica gel in your box can help reduce general dampness.

Check the split rings. It's amazing how many expensive lures are fitted with steel or bronze split rings. Change these for stainless-steel ones, which are available if you look around.

Check that the eye and hook mountings are secure. Many quality lures, especially wooden ones, have an internal harness to which the hook attachment points are connected, and lures made like this will not give any trouble. Some lures have hooks held on rings screwed into the body. These are fine, but check that they screw in really firmly; if in doubt, remove them, add a drop of Araldite to the thread and refix them. Finally, check that vanes are not loose or bent.

As far as finish is concerned, cracks in wooden lures should be sealed over to prevent water seepage. A coat of varnish will do it. Hollow lures should be checked for puncture holes and repaired. Scratched paint finishes are honourable scars, and will almost certainly not affect a lure's catching capability.

Famous Names, but Long Gone

The sharp-eyed reader will notice that a lot of very famous lures aren't included in our guide. Where is the Gudebrod Sniper? Where is the Heddon Lucky 13? The answer is, long gone out of production. Much has been written about these lures of yesterday, and many people wonder why such good lures should disappear. The truth is that making lures is a commercial exercise, and as in all manufacturing processes, when sales of a model decline, that model will be discontinued.

Sadly, it's goodbye to the lures mentioned above. They are now museum pieces in the hands of collectors.

Lures come and go, but types and categories live on. New lures appear every year and sometimes old lures reappear under different manufacturers' names.

When developing your lure armoury, you will probably find one or two lures of particular colours and patterns which you like very much and prove deadly for your water. If you're using them regularly, you're probably losing them a lot. But what if your favourites are discontinued? The only answer to the problem of disappearing brands is to buy a small supply of the lures you like and hide them under the floorboards against the day when you can't buy them any more!

Collecting Lures

It's possible to spend a small fortune on lures, and many anglers get a great deal of enjoyment from building a collection of lures which they may use only occasionally for fishing, if ever! As time goes by, lures which get discontinued may become collector's items, and even become quite valuable. It's fun to spot future treasures, and also to have a collection of old 'war horses', honourably retired from the tackle box whether rare or not.

In recent years, well known lures like River Runt (Heddon), Lucky 13 (Heddon), Wiggle Fish (Creek Chub), Sniper (Gudebrod) and many more have become collector's items. Others will follow, but which ones? After all, many of the rarest lures were big sellers in their day. Here are a few ideas:

● **Wooden lures**. Most modern lures are made of plastic, polycarbonate or foam. Wooden lures are in decline, and the appeal of nostalgia should be considered.

● Very **large** or very **small** examples of a particular lure. There are always fewer of these made, and so they will always be rarer.

● **Unusual colours**. For every one lure sold in Rainbow Sky Blue Pink, there will probably be a hundred sold in Perch or Shad.

● Lures with **unusual features** or gimmicks which are bound not to catch on.

● Good quality lures made by very **small companies**.

You could choose a theme for a collection, say one of every lure produced by a certain manufacturer, or only lures of a certain colour, or all the lures available in the year you were born. These are just a few thoughts on the subject, and if you're a natural collector you won't need any more convincing! Just one last point, remember to keep all packaging, catalogues, photographs and articles about your lures. These will add both value and interest to your collection.

CHAPTER TWO
SURFACE LURES

This category consists of lures such as Crawlers and other floating lures which are not intended to dive or sink below the surface.

Such lures tend to be imitations of frogs (e.g. Buzz'n Frog) or mice (e.g. Bassrat). Most predatory fish will feed off small frogs, voles, ducklings, worms and anything else live and edible which is careless enough to be found on the water.

This kind of food tends to be found in and around heavy weed growth or overhanging vegetation, which, along with shelter and protection, is why predators tend to lurk in such areas. These are, of course, the best areas to fish.

Surface lures are at their most effective in the summer months, particularly at dawn and dusk. Snatching the odd hour here and there for fishing is what most working people can expect, and it's sessions with surface lures during these brief hours which have provided us with some of the most enjoyable sport we've had on our local small pike water.

Look for weedless lures (with either single hooks raised up proud of the lure, protected hooks or weed guards on the lure itself) for fishing in the middle of lily beds where the pike and perch think they are safe!

Noisy lures like the Crazy Crawler and the Jitterbug perform well fished across the mouth of very small shallow bays. Use a medium-speed retrieve for these two lures, and keep them away from surface weed, which will quickly foul them up and spoil their action.

———— ◆ ————

Bassrat   *PLATE N*

Manufacturer   Southern Lure Co, USA

Classification   Surface lure

Construction   Soft, hollow-bodied lure with a double hook which fits around the body. Slim rat shape, multi-strand skirt.

Colours/finish   Fourteen colours, ranging from natural to fluorescent.

Sizes   Available in one size only: 60mm long, 10g weight.

Use   Completely weedless. Bassrat can be fished on the top of thick weed, allowing it to skitter over lilies and drop into gaps between the pads. Over open water, fish with short jerks to make it dart and bob like a swimming rat. Check the lure every now and again to make sure the body is still fitting snugly against the hooks to retain its weedless qualities.

Others to try   **Thundertoad** (Southern Lure, USA).

Buzz'n Frog   *PLATE N*

Manufacturer   Rebel, USA

Classification   Surface lure

Construction   Represents a frog with rear

legs spinning around a central axis. Equipped with a double hook made weedless by the action of the legs.

Colours/finish Four colour options, all 'froggie' shades from dark green to yellow with natural frog pattern.

Sizes Available in one size: 76mm long, 14g weight.

Use A good, noisy surface lure ideal for waters with a good population of frogs. The lure throws up a wave of water as it is retrieved. Particularly useful for attracting pike lurking in heavy weed beds and amongst lilies. Great fun to use.

Others to try No comparable hard baits, but several soft plastic frogs are available. See also **Wee Frog** (Rebel, USA).

Crazy Crawler   *PLATE N*

Manufacturer Heddon, USA

Classification Surface lure

Construction Tubby plastic, slightly frog-like body, with hinged wings or paddles. Two treble hooks, large painted eyes.

Colours/finish Seven colour options, the favourites being the yellow and red hornet pattern and the bullfrog version, though they will all catch.

Sizes Two sizes: the standard 60mm long, 17.5g weight, and the Tiny Crawler, 45mm long, 7g weight.

Use Britain's biggest selling surface lure by far. Crazy Crawler paddles through the water on retrieve, creating a splashing commotion rather like a demented duckling. Speed of

retrieve is important – too slow, and the crawler won't crawl properly. Opinion seems divided on the Crazy Crawler. Most people love it and catch a lot of fish with it, others say they've never succeeded with it. We suspect that it works better in coloured water, when fish respond to the sound, and less well if they can see it. At least it's fun to use, and has cheered up many a dull session for us, often by presenting us with a pike! The Tiny Crawler has accounted for some excellent pike, perch and even chub. Designed over 50 years ago (originally called the Jersey Wow), this is a lure you should definitely try at least once.

Others to try There are copies available in the US, but Crazy Crawler is really out on its own.

Jitterbug   *PLATE N*

Manufacturer Arbogast, USA

Classification Surface crawler

Construction Wooden body, large painted eyes, characteristic double-lobed popping lip, two trebles (three on largest version). Jointed, rattling and weedless versions are also available; the weedless version has a rubber skirt.

Colours/finish Fifteen colour options, including some superb yellows and coachdogs. Darker patterns such as Bass are recommended for night fishing.

Sizes Eight sizes ranging from 32mm long, 7g weight to 114mm long, 35g weight.

Use One of the noisiest surface lures around, the Jitterbug has been in the top three best-selling lures in the US since before World War II. For many people it's a 'banker' amongst surface lures.

Others to try   There really isn't an alternative for this classic, although the **Jitterstick** offers a larger and noisier variation.

Jitterstick   *PLATE N*

Manufacturer   Arbogast, USA

Classification   Surface crawler

Construction   Cigar-shaped plug with large double-lobed lip and tail prop. Two treble hooks.

Colours/finish   Twelve colours, predominantly mixtures of black, white and yellow. Perch and Yellow Coachdog are favourites.

Sizes   Two sizes: 89mm long, 11g weight; 102mm long, 18g weight.

Use   A stretched version of the standard Jitterbug designed to create more surface disturbance. As well as being longer, the Jitterstick has a large tail propeller which adds to the plopping sound produced by the lobed lip as it wobbles through the water. Probably a bit too noisy to use on a very calm day when it may scare the fish, but worth trying when there is a chop on the water.

Others to try   **Jitterbug** (Arbogast, USA).

Natural Frog   *PLATE N*

Manufacturer   Renowsky, USA

Classification   Surface lure

Construction   Soft rubber lifelike imitation frog with large single weed-guarded hook.

Colours/finish   Two colours, green and brown, with frog pattern.

Sizes   One size only: 90mm long, 14g weight.

Use   A handy lure for fishing holes in weed beds, flopping off lily pads, swimming along the edge of rush beds, and generally 'thinking frog' with. Fish sink and draw, slowly, making the frog's legs work. Virtually weedless.

Others to try   **Frog Bait** (Burke, USA).

Scum Frog   *PLATE N*

Manufacturer   Southern Lure Co, USA

Classification   Surface lure

Construction   A hollow, soft plastic weedless plug with a double hook mounted to fit snugly around the body. Trailing multi-coloured vinyl skirt. Comes with adjustable trailer hook.

Colours/finish   Fourteen colour options, including four fluorescent colours and three spotty finishes.

Sizes   Standard (55mm long, 9g weight) and Junior (40mm long, 7g weight) Scum Frog version available.

Use   The ideal lure for popping slowly back through lilies and other surface vegetation. Can be made to emit loud popping noises by a series of jerks on a slow retrieve. The big plus with this lure is its absolutely weedless design. You can really take liberties, throwing it into places where other lures would get hopelessly snagged up. Be prepared to have these lures shredded to bits by enthusiastic pike.

Others to try   **Scumfrog Popper** (Southern Lure Co, USA) – designed as a popper. **Two Tiny Toads** (Southern Lure Co, USA) – two tiny frogs on the same trace.

Rattlin' Rat (Manns, USA).
Swimming Frog (Manns, USA).

Wee Frog   *PLATE N*

Manufacturer   Rebel, USA

Classification   Surface lure (though technically a floating diver)

Construction   A natural frog-shaped lure with bulging froggy eyes; inset plastic lip, two trebles attached by split rings.

Colours/finish   Four colours: natural frog colours from chartreuse to dark green.

Sizes   Two sizes: 50mm length, 10g weight and Teeny-Wee Frog 38mm length, 3.5g weight.

Use   Fish around floating vegetation with a stop-start action to attract fish waiting in ambush. Although it can dive, it really seems to work best as a twitched surface lure around the lily pads. Will be taken by pike, perch and perhaps a 'lunker' chub if you're lucky!

Others to try   Buzz'n Frog (Rebel, USA).

———— ♦ ————

Chuggers

Chuggers are surface plugs which all have concave or indented front surfaces. This creates uneven water pressure as the lure is retrieved, giving rise to chugging sounds, and many chuggers will even pop and spit water when twitched hard across the surface. As a group, they are easy to cast, simple and enjoyable to use, and very productive in the spring

and summer months, especially early in the morning and at the end of the day.

Some chuggers can be made to dive a few inches below the surface by using a fast or jerky retrieve. All give good surface water disturbance, sending out vibrations which fish will pick up and investigate. They are designed to imitate small creatures on the surface, injured fish, frogs and so on, and this should be borne in mind when using them. Cast the lure out, and let it rest until the ripples die away. Then give it one or two short twitches; at this point, the lure will often be taken in a spectacular swirl of sparkling water and silver fish. This is always the first thing we do when fishing a summer pike water, and it pays off very frequently. A chugger can be cast parallel to the bank ahead and twitched slowly back, you can use it to hunt around weed beds, pontoons and moored boats. Just 'think fish' and the ideas will come.

The danger with chuggers is that they're so much fun to use that you can get carried away and concentrate on making them pop really loudly, or spit lots of water. It's a mistake to think that the louder the pop, the better you're doing. Reserve the really spectacular effects for days when there's a bit of ripple or chop on the water, when you need the loud noises and fountains of splashing to attract the fish. On a calm day or when the water is very clear, go for the less dramatic lures and a gentler twitching technique; loud noises in conditions like these may actually spook the fish you're trying to attract.

Finally, as with all surface lures, check that the weight of your wire trace is not sinking your lure and inhibiting its action. If it is, shorten your trace to around 12in and replace the snap swivel with a snap only. This is particularly important with small floating lures of all kinds.

———— ♦ ————

Bass Oreno   *PLATE L*

Manufacturer Luhr-Jensen, USA

Classification Surface chugger

Construction Oblique scooped-out frontal surface, made of wood, two trebles.

Colours/finish Ten colours; good range of standard patterns including Black Bass, Frog and the well thought of Red Head.

Sizes Three sizes: 60mm long, 11g weight; 70mm long, 14g weight; 90mm long, 18g weight.

Use A classic lure, originally manufactured by South Bend (USA). The Bass Oreno can be twitched under the surface to pop back up again in almost the same place, making it ideal for situations where a very slow retrieve is wanted. To vary the pattern, a sharp jerk will cause the plug to pop and splash before darting under.

Blabbermouth   *PLATE L*

Manufacturer Gudebrod Inc, USA

Classification Surface chugger

Construction Standard popper shape with tapering tail. The head is scooped and cut away at an angle in 'slider' style. Tail prop, large eyes, two trebles.

Colours/finish Six colours, high quality scale-type finishes.

Sizes Two sizes: 75mm long, 14g weight; 50mm long, 4g weight.

Use A quiet slider-style popper designed for use on calm days in clear, shallow water

where fish may be easily spooked. Practise fishing with short twitches, using the rod tip to give it live action in the water. Makes a 'plip plip' sound because of the combination of face shape and propeller. Another great lure for early mornings and summer evenings.

Hula Popper   *PLATE L*

Manufacturer Arbogast, USA

Classification Surface chugger

Construction The Hula Popper has the characteristic concave front of the true popper. The smaller versions have a single treble hook, the larger have two. All have a vinyl 'hula' skirt to give movement even when the lure is at rest.

Colours/finish Fifteen standard colours; Yellow Frog is a particular favourite.

Sizes Four sizes: 32mm long, 5g weight; 44mm long, 7g weight; 51mm long, 11g weight; 57mm long, 18g weight.

Use Around since 1941. At its best on the edge of weed beds or coming back through thin rushes, Hula Popper can be made to emit very loud popping noises and plenty of underwater bubbles as it comes back. One of the noisiest poppers around.

Others to try Pop R (Rebel, USA).
Chug Bug (Storm, USA).
Trouble Maker (Gudebrod, USA).

Mirrolure Jointed Surface Popper   *PLATE L*

Manufacturer Mirrolure, USA

Classification Surface chugger

Construction Jointed lure with big head and small tail, slightly wedge-shaped concave mouth, prominent fishy eyes, two trebles. In a variant version the rear treble is dressed with a black and white bucktail.

Colours/finish Mirrolure offer some of the most attractive finishes around, and they stand up well to wear and tear. The Jointed Popper comes in 36 colours – one for every situation.

Sizes Available in one size only: 73mm long, 10.5g weight.

Use An interesting variation on the popper theme, this lure can be fished equally effectively at a variety of speeds. Has a nice wiggle, and a big pop when fished at slower speeds. Said to take sea trout, it's better known in the UK as a summer pike lure, and we suspect (no proof yet!) that chub like it too.

Pencil Popper   *PLATE L*

Manufacturer Cordell, USA

Classification Surface chugger

Construction A large, tail-weighted floating popping lure, tapered towards the head; concave face, small moulded eyes. Two heavy-duty saltwater trebles are attached with split rings.

Colours/finish Seven colours, mainly combinations including silver or pearl.

Sizes Two sizes: 178mm long, 56g weight; 153mm long, 28g weight.

Use An extremely long-casting floating surf lure. The tail is weighted to force the tail in the direction of the cast, meaning it doesn't tumble in the air. The lure lands tail down,

offering an immediate target. Retrieve with long jerks. Designed for saltwater, but could also be used for pike on big waters.

Others to try **Prancer** (Arbogast, USA). **Dasher** (Arbogast, USA).

PJ Pop   *PLATE L*

Manufacturer Luhr-Jensen, USA

Classification Surface chugger

Construction Cured sugar pine body, large carved eyes, cupped face, two well secured treble hooks, the rear one dressed with a tinsel bucktail – top quality.

Colours/finish Thirteen colours, Rainbow Trout is particularly nice looking.

Sizes Two sizes: 60mm long, 5g weight; 80mm long, 11g weight.

Use A spitting popper; as it is jerked across the surface of the water, the scooped-out face catches water which it spits out with a popping sound. Try dead-sticking it: cast it out and wait for the ripples to die down before giving it two quick pops; wait 30 seconds then repeat. This method is very effective in the spring and summer when fish are feeding very actively. One of Luhr Jensen's top sellers, this very versatile lure can also be retrieved fast or even by walking the dog. Well worth experimenting with. Designed by Phil Jensen (son of Luhr), hence the name.

Pop-R   *PLATE L*

Manufacturer Rebel, USA

Classification Surface chugger

21

Construction Conventional popper shape with concave face to produce the characteristic popping noise on retrieve. Two trebles, the rear one dressed with a bucktail, attached with split rings.

Colours/finish Seventeen colours: our favourite is Red Eye Perch.

Sizes Three sizes: 51mm long, 3.5g weight; 57mm long, 7g weight; 76mm long, 14g weight.

Use This lure will take pike, perch, even chub on its day. Use early and late season, fish fast when fish are moving, more slowly on duller days. One of Rebel's best known lures, a proven killer.

Others to try Hula Popper (Arbogast, USA).

Saltwater Bug PLATE L

Manufacturer Gaines Phillips, USA

Classification Surface chugger

Construction Balsa wood tapered plug with flat raked face, painted eyes, single-dressed 2/0 hook.

Colours/finish Ten colours; simple combinations of blue, pearl, black, yellow and red.

Sizes One size: 28mm long, 1.5g weight.

Use Designed for use with a flyrod, but can also be used with light spinning tackle. Tweak across the water in classic popper style. Despite their small size, they are intended for heavy duty use for large surface-feeding fish in the sea (such as tarpon), and will also take game fish, pike, perch and chub. Small lures like

this need to be fished with the shortest and lightest possible wire trace or they cannot develop their action.

Others to try Gaines Phillips have a wide range of **Popping Bugs**, worth looking at if this style of fishing interests you.

Scudder PLATE L

Manufacturer Arbogast, USA

Classification Surface chugger

Construction Large wooden popping bait, very deep concave head. Wired through, large ring-type line connector. Two heavy-duty 3X treble hooks, big painted eye.

Colours/finish Six good colours. Blue Mackerel with Chartreuse sides is particularly attractive.

Sizes Three sizes: 102mm long, 28g weight; 114mm long, 42g weight, 127mm long, 56g weight.

Use A very tough sea lure, a floating popper to use in the surf. The very noisy pop is good for calling up fish when they don't seem very active. Can be tiring to use because of its size and action. Recommended for exotics like tarpon and barracuda, but worth a try for early morning bass perhaps?

Silver Sides PLATE L

Manufacturer Gaines Phillips, USA

Classification Surface chugger

Construction Simple plug shape with a plain flat-sloped face. With 300lb test hi-tensile strength stainless steel wired through the body, the belly hook is also attached to this by a wire loop. Two cadmium-plated trebles.

Colours/finish Twelve colours, including a couple of good blues and silver based versions which are worth trying in the sea.

Sizes Two sizes: 127mm long, 35g weight; 101mm long, 24.5g weight.

Use A surface lure designed especially for salt water, but could, of course, be used in freshwater. A slow, steady retrieve will produce a smooth swimming action; a more erratic retrieve will make the lure skip across the water. This is quite a heavy plug, so don't go mad with it when conditions are very still, as there's a danger of spooking the fish. Gaines specialize in very strongly constructed lures, and this one will certainly stand up to a battering.

Soft Classic Pop-R   *PLATE L*

Manufacturer Soft Classic, USA

Classification Sinking surface chugger

Construction Soft plastic (the consistency of a wine gum) plug with dished face and tapered tail. Rigged with a Heddon Excaliber offset hook (one supplied in each pack of three lures).

Colours/finish Five colours, all with metallic flecks. Colours of these soft plastic lures can vary slightly from batch to batch. Chartreuse Pepper looks particularly good.

Sizes One size: 65mm long, 10g weight.

Use This lure can be worked on the surface using short jerking motions like a conventional popper; it can be made to pop and spit very easily. When the retrieve is halted (which it always should be after a fish strikes short), the lure will sink slowly and hopefully stimulate another strike. Can be fished in, around and through weed with no problem – it really is weedless, as the hook point is buried in the soft body of the lure. New to the UK in 1993, and looks like an interesting variation on the surface lure theme.

Others to try The original **Pop-R** (Rebel, USA) hard plastic bait on which this is based.

Striper Striker   *PLATE L*

Manufacturer Creek Chub, USA

Classification Sinking chugger

Construction Solid plastic with small moulded eyes and concave chugger face. Wired through, two heavy-duty trebles attached with split rings; the belly treble is anchored to a swivel which prevents large fish using the lure body to lever themselves off the hook. The rear treble is dressed with a white bucktail.

Colours/finish Seven colours, all pale; most popular are the Metallic Silver and the Blue Flash.

Sizes Four sizes: 76mm long, 7g weight; 90mm long, 21g weight; 108mm long, 42g weight; 127mm long, 60.5g weight.

Use Primarily a saltwater lure, holds the World Striper Record at 66lb. Remember this is a sinking lure, and so start working it the instant it hits the water. A fast, continuous retrieve, varying the speed, will make the lure jitter and jump just like a bait fish. Very long casting, recommended for boat and surf casting. Reported to be a good tarpon lure, worth a try for summer bass.

Others to try The large sizes of **Trouble-maker** (Gudebrod Inc, USA).

Troublemaker
PLATE L

Manufacturer Gudebrod Inc, USA

Classification Surface chugger

Construction Standard popper shape with concave face and tapered tail, large moulded eyes, two trebles, the tail treble either plain or dressed with a bucktail.

Colours/finish Six colours available including three mackerel-type patterns in black, red and yellow.

Sizes Available in five sizes ranging from the 140mm long, 56g weight sea version down to a 4g baby.

Use When fished with a short sharp jerk, the Troublemaker can be made to spit a shower of droplets a good 18in in front of it, creating the impression of a shower of fry bursting from the water and arousing the curiosity of hunting predators. A successful lure for chub, as well as pike and perch. A very high quality example of the surface poppers used extensively for bass in the USA.

Others to try **Wood Chug** (Smithwick, USA).

Chapter Three
Propbaits

Propbaits are floating lures which have propeller blades either at the head or the tail – or in many cases at both ends. Their action is said to replicate the sounds made by distressed fish. These are top-water lures, some of which can be jerked into diving a few inches.

They are amongst the noisiest of surface lures, creating a big churned-up wake of water: they are the ones to choose when the water is ruffled up or very coloured. They are less easy to cast accurately than some of the other categories of surface lure.

The twin-prop versions (one at each end) create the most noise and disturbance of all, and are effective when used with a fast twitching retrieve which will really get the props turning. At maximum speed some propbaits, like the Heddon Torpedo, almost 'sing', so it's easy to tell when you're fishing them at optimum speed.

When buying a Propbait (and indeed any lure with a spinner), check to make sure that the props are free running. You should keep a close check on the propellers, particularly if you're fishing a weedy swim, to make sure that little bits of silk weed haven't got twisted up in them. The blades can be tuned if you are not happy with the way they spin; both angle and pitch can be altered.

By weighting the line (or using a downrigger in deep water) Propbaits can be used with success at depth.

——— ◆ ———

Boy Howdy   *PLATE N*

Manufacturer   Cordell, USA

Classification   Propbait

Construction   A long slim lure with props fore and aft. Moulded eyes, three trebles (two belly, one tail), attached with split rings.

Colours/finish   Eight colours, including four metallics. Favourites are Frog and Gold/Black.

Sizes   One size: 114mm long, 11g weight.

Use   A good spring lure for pike, particularly effective when cast over feeding fish, as it imitates an injured fish. Use a smooth, steady retrieve in calm water, an erratic retrieve in choppy water.

Others to try   Devil's Horse (Smithwick, USA).
Dying Flutter (Heddon, USA).

Crazy Shad   *PLATE N*

Manufacturer   Cordell, USA

Classification   Propbait

Construction   Plastic body, small moulded eyes, front and rear propeller (the same as those of the Boy Howdy), two trebles, attached with split rings.

Colours/finish Eight colours, including four metallics. The favourite is probably the unusual Clear/Blue Nose.

Sizes Just one size in production: 76mm long, 21g weight.

Use A basic style propbait, easy to cast and use. Retrieve with a hesitant action, varying the speed and occasionally stopping completely. Readily taken by pike early and late season.

Others to try Sinner Spinner (Gudebrod, USA).

Crippled Killer   *PLATE N*

Manufacturer Gaines Phillips, USA

Classification Propbait

Construction Squat plastic body tapered at each end; prominent painted eye. Counter-rotating props fore and aft. Two treble hooks.

Colours/finish Twenty-four colours ranging from transparent to black; a wide choice of naturals and bright, including nine with special glow finish.

Sizes Four sizes: Big Crippled Killer: 90mm long, 14g weight; Original Crippled Killer: 57mm long, 7g weight; Baby Crippled Killer: 51mm long, 3.5g weight; Midget Crippled Killer: 51mm long, 7g weight.

Use A very popular top-water lure which has been around for over 50 years. A very splashy propbait in a useful range of sizes, good for days when the surface is a bit ruffled. Crippled Killers are conventional floaters except for the Midget, which is a fast-sinking version useful for days when the fish won't take from the surface.

Dasher   *PLATE N*

Manufacturer Arbogast, USA

Classification Propbait

Construction Wooden construction with a high gloss finish. Fore and aft props, three vast trebles (the front one rather unnecessary perhaps, whilst the other two need replacing with something a little smaller – though some may disagree).

Colours/finish Six good catching colours, including a super Perch Glitter, Blue Mackerel, red and white and fluorescent orange/ yellow.

Sizes Available in two sizes: 152mm long, 28g weight, and a mighty 178mm long, 63g version.

Use Primarily intended as a saltwater lure, the Dasher will interest those who are looking for a really big surface lure for use on productive summer shallows. Very suitable for surface-feeding bass as well as the many exotic sport fish which will take this lure. Named for some mysterious reason (along with its stable-mate the Prancer) after one of Father Christmas's reindeer.

Devil's Horse   *PLATE N*

Manufacturer Smithwick, USA

Classification Propbait

Construction High buoyancy wooden cigar-shaped lure, two belly trebles secured with metal plates plus a tail treble (except the 7g size which has just one belly treble plus tail treble). Leaf-bladed props fore and aft, large painted eyes.

Colours/finish   Twenty-eight colours, including six Sunburst colours which have a glittering finish currently fashionable with US manufacturers. Good performers include Silver Shiner and Perch.

Sizes   A range of four sizes: The Devil's Horse Dancer: 83mm long, 7g weight; and also 89mm, 11g weight; 115mm long, 14g weight; 140mm, 18g weight.

Use   First introduced in the 1940s the Devil's Horse has a long pedigree and is one of the most popular propbaits made. It is a medium loud lure, very strongly constructed with quality hardware. This lure imitates an injured baitfish. Cast it at a swirling fish, and it will often be fooled into thinking that the lure is a fish it has struck and crippled. Can be used in calm or slightly choppy water.

Dying Flutter   *PLATE N*

Manufacturer   Heddon, USA

Classification   Propbait

Construction   Cigar-shaped plastic body with angled prop blades fore and aft. Two trebles, the belly treble fixed by a metal plate. Painted eyes.

Colours/finish   Nine colours, mainly 'broken' patterns which may camouflage the lures's outline. The Clear option works particularly well at night.

Sizes   One size: 95mm long, 10g weight.

Use   A million-plus selling lure which should be fished with short ripping jerks for maximum effect. The propellers make a loud whirring noise, stimulating attack. Try this lure in clear water, where you can see signs of pike hunting.

Others to try   Devil's Horse (Smithwick, USA).

Nip-I-Diddee   *PLATE N*

Manufacturer   Luhr-Jensen, USA

Classification   Propbait

Construction   Cigar-shaped wooden lure with front and rear mounted props, two trebles, large painted eyes.

Colours/finish   Fourteen colour options, mainly naturals. Very high gloss finish – Yellow Spotted Pup is a favourite.

Sizes   Available in three sizes: 55mm long, 7g weight; 65mm long, 11g weight; 80mm long, 18g weight.

Use   Highly buoyant surface wooden lure which has been around a long time. Fish very slowly off the edge of cover such as weed beds and lily pads. Allowing the lure to rest and then twitching will often provoke a strike. Luhr-Jensen acquired Nip-I-Diddee (like Bass Oreno) from South Bend, who in turn had bought them from Glen Evans Inc, the original manufacturers. Another possible future collector's item?

Panatella   *PLATE N*

Manufacturer   Luhr-Jensen, USA

Classification   Propbait

Construction   Slim cigar-shaped body made from cured sugar pine, radical pitch stainless steel prop fore and aft, two trebles.

Colours/finish   Thirteen colours, the Silver Foil/Black Shad version looks particularly good, as does the Yellow with Black/Red Spots.

Sizes   Two sizes: 85mm long, 10.5g weight; 100mm long, 14g weight.

Use   The Panatella is pretty much a slimmer version of the Luhr-Jensen Woodchopper. The props are very free turning, and respond to very small movements, which are often all that's needed when fishing surface lures. Fish this slowly, in a succession of small twitches, or cast it out and leave it for a minute or two before beginning a slow, hesitating retrieve. Try fishing it parallel to the bank ahead of you; a good option for early season pike.

Sinner Spinner   *PLATE N*

Manufacturer   Gudebrod, USA

Classification   Propbait

Construction   Chubby cigar-shaped lure with small props fore and aft. Two trebles, large moulded eyes.

Colours/finish   Like all Gudebrod lures, beautiful reflective surfaces are coated with clear Lexan for a tough, non-chip colour finish.

Sizes   Three sizes: 70mm long, 14g weight; 62mm long, 7g weight; 45mm long, 4g weight.

Use   Beautifully finished, the Sinner Spinner is straight out of Barrie Rickards Top Ten all-time favourites. Tends to lie on its side during retrieve, imitating the disturbed movements and shiny flanks of an injured baitfish, creating a wide ripple on the surface. A relatively quiet surface lure, good for use in very calm water, and particularly recommended for chub.

Others to try   **Surface Spinner** (Mirrolure, USA).

Torpedo   *PLATE N*

Manufacturer   Heddon, USA

Classification   Propbait

Construction   Cigar-shaped lure with rear-mounted prop and two trebles.

Colours/finish   Eighteen colour patterns are offered plus six in G-Finish and two in G-Fleck.

Sizes   Three sizes available: Baby Torpedo, 64mm long, 11g weight; Tiny Torpedo, 48mm long, 7g weight; and Teeny Torpedo, 38mm long, 4g weight.

Use   Torpedo is one of the great classic surface lures. It's very easy to use, and particularly easy to cast accurately. Though basically a surface lure, it can also be ripped a few inches sub-surface. When it is retrieved fast, it emits a singing noise which provokes strikes, while a slower retrieve gives plenty of splash and a different, lower vibration.

Others to try   **Crazy Shad** (Cordell, USA). **Woodchopper** (Luhr-Jensen, USA).

Woodchopper   *PLATE N*

Manufacturer   Luhr-Jensen, USA

Classification   Propbait

Construction   One of the much admired Ozark Mountain lures, handcrafted from sugar pine, giving good buoyancy characteristics and a superb finish. Fore and after mounted radical pitch stainless-steel props, a dumpy body and a prominent eye make this a very good-looking lure.

Performance A surface lure which creates considerable disturbance with its two props, both imitating a wounded fish and setting up attracting vibrations.

Colours/finish Thirteen colours offered, including a superb Red Head, a good-looking Rainbow Trout and a traditional (in the US, that is) Yellow/Black/Red Combo.

Sizes Available in three sizes: 55mm long, 11g weight; 80mm long, 14g weight; 105mm long, 21g weight.

Use Like many surface lures, this one is effective when cast towards a swirling fish, deceiving the quarry into striking at an apparently injured bait fish.

Others to try Panatella (Luhr-Jensen, USA): slightly slimmer version, same great finish and big eye.

CHAPTER FOUR
STICKBAITS AND JERKBAITS

Technically, stickbaits are lipless, floating lures which do not dive or have any built-in action of their own. Jerkbaits, on the other hand, are generally larger, and tend to have shaped noses (but again, no diving vane), so they will dive on retrieve. We have bracketed these types together, because the differences between them are not great and their working methods are quite similar. Besides, there are relatively few of these lures easily available on the UK market.

The function of a diving vane is to guide the flow of water in a single direction, so that a lure will be pushed down through the water. The principle is similar to that of the air uplift which helps an aircraft take off. If a lure has no vane, it will move forward in the water in a random fashion, perhaps to the right, perhaps to the left, and up and down.

You achieve this effect with a stickbait by retrieving the lure in a twitching jerk, pausing until the lure stops, then repeating the same action over and over again. This will make the lure move erratically from side to side; a fast succession of jerks will produce a succession of lure movements to one side, i.e. it will track to the left or track to the right, but the movements will still be erratic and darting. This technique is known as 'walking the dog', and it's a very popular style of retrieve in the US. It takes some practice (try it with an easy lure at first: a Zara Spook or Soft Classic Zara Puppy). The effect you are trying to produce is that of a darting fish. With practice, you'll find that you can make some stickbaits operate 'on the spot', looking like a bait fish feeding on the surface. (We have seen Mervyn

Jones do this with a Bill Lewis Slapstick, and attract a shoal of living fish around the lure, so convincing was the action he was creating. Skills like this are not common, but *are* achievable with practice.)

Jerkbaits are in some respects the stickbait's big brother. Because of their size, they create a lot of disturbance as they displace water; it is probably this which attracts the hunting predator.

Jerkbaits are fished with a series of jerks; the harder the jerk, the deeper the dive. A rapid succession of jerks will take the lure to its maximum depth. They are designed to imitate a wounded fish, and although some of these lures look a bit like a piece of firewood your eight-year-old painted and brought home from school, don't be deceived – in the water, and with a bit of practice, you can make them look remarkably lifelike in their action. Some jerkbaits have a metal tail, and you should experiment with its effect on the lure's performance by changing the angle (by bending the tail up and down) and the shape (by pinching it in). In order to gain greater depth, many enthusiasts add weight to jerkbaits by loading them with lead, but we'd suggest you try them unloaded first, to get used to the action and what they can do.

Jerkbaits are not for the absolute beginner, but they have been very successful in the UK in the hands of some of the leading lure anglers, and we will undoubtedly be hearing more about them in the future.

——— ◆ ———

Dalton Special
PLATE M

Manufacturer   Luhr-Jensen, USA

Classification   Jerkbait

Construction   Wooden surface lure with a very prominent eye.

Colours/finish   Nine standard colour patterns. Perch and Little Bass particularly recommended. Very high quality varnish finish.

Sizes   Available in three sizes: 70mm long, 9g weight; 80mm long, 11g weight; 105mm long, 21g weight.

Use   Can be used walking-the-dog style, and in a sharp jerk/pause routine. Good for 'dead-sticking' when the lure is cast out and left until the surface splash dies away. The lure is then twitched a few feet, left for dead again, and the process is repeated until the lure is fully retrieved.

Others to try   Jerk'n Sam (Luhr-Jensen, USA).

Gaines' Flipper
PLATE I

Manufacturer   Gaines Phillips, USA

Classification   Stickbait

Construction   Lipless plug with a single-size 2/0 treble hook, two-thirds of the way along the body. Rigged through the body with 300lb test wire; red bead at nose and tail; diamond-shaped metal tail. Painted eyes.

Colours/finish   Twelve colours, mainly in themes of blue, yellow and black, including two with a luminous glow. Black with a red flash is our favourite.

Sizes   One size: 102mm long, 21g weight.

Use   This plug is most effective fished walking-the-dog style; it will dart and dive with ease. Retrieved with a jerking action, it will get down to 2 ft. The metal tail produces a slight quiver in the lure as it comes to rest. Designed for big, strong fish, we use it for late-season pike in shallow waters. Also recommended for tarpon.

Others to try   **Top Gun** (Bagley, USA). **Zara Spook** (Heddon, USA).

Highroller
PLATE M

Manufacturer   Smithwick, USA

Classification   Stickbait

Construction   Wooden cigar-shaped lure; two treble hooks, good painted eyes underneath the body.

Colours/finish   Five attractive colours; the favourite is probably Perch.

Sizes   Two sizes: 105mm long, 14g weight; 80mm long, 7g weight.

Use   This surface lure is designed to be twitched across the top of the water; it can also be twitched in place. The action is a little like that of the Zara Spook, though it's perhaps slightly easier to get the right action with the Highroller because of the way it's balanced in the water.

Others to try   **Zara Spook** (Heddon, USA).

Jerk'n Sam
PLATE M

Manufacturer   Luhr-Jensen, USA

31

Classification Stickbait

Construction Slim wooden plug with V-cut face, large painted eyes, tail prop and two treble hooks, the rear hook dressed with a white bucktail.

Colours/finish A limited but attractive range of eight colours, including two foil finishes. High quality glossy finish.

Sizes Three sizes: 90mm long, 12g weight; 85mm long, 7g weight; 75mm long, 5g weight.

Use This is a noisy lure, creating plenty of vibration with a combination of propeller and shaped head. Use a jerking, twitching retrieve and fish around likely holding spots. It is also effective cast out and left for a minute or two before moving it (dead-sticking) – this often provokes an immediate strike. Good when the water is a little choppy.

Jumping Snooker *PLATE M*

Manufacturer Arbogast, USA

Classification Stickbait

Construction Wooden minnow-shaped lure with flattened head, rear-weighted so that it floats almost vertically with its nose sticking out of the water. Beautifully finished wooden body; two Mustad treble hooks attached with split ring.

Sizes Three sizes: 89mm long, 11g weight; 114mm long, 14g weight; 140mm long, 21g weight.

Use The Jumping Snooker is best fished in walking-the-dog fashion, when it will dart and weave and behave very much like a real fish. Very sharp twitches can actually bring the lure right out of the water, resembling a fish

being chased by a predator. A good example of a stickbait, it is very useful when predators are observed hitting surface fry shoals.

Mirrolure Classic 52MR *PLATE M*

Manufacturer Mirrolure, USA

Classification Stickbait

Construction Lipless plug with large naturalistic eyes and three treble hooks. Encapsulated reflective finish.

Colours/finish Thirty-six colour schemes, scratch resistant, mainly single-body reflective colours. The Sardine, Rudd and Perch finishes are very attractive and good catchers. What Mirrolures lack in imaginative colour combinations they make up for in the quality of colour finish – amongst the best available on the market today.

Sizes Six versions are available (plus two with rattles): 92mm long, 14g weight (depth 1–4ft+); 92mm long, 14g weight (depth 3–8ft+);92mm long, 17.5g weight (depth 4–9ft+); 92mm long, 24.5g weight (depth 5–10ft+); 108mm long, 24.5g weight (depth 3–7ft+);108mm long, 35g weight (depth 5–10ft+).

Use This well-known slow-sinking stickbait can be jerked down to its operating depth in a series of short or long sweeps, after which it rises slowly up in the water, when it is twitched down again. The Mirrolure enables you to search out an area very thoroughly; it is used widely for saltwater gamefish in the US. Has recently started to attract attention in the UK not only as a sea lure, but also for medium-deep water piking. Under-used as a freshwater lure, it seems likely that Mirrolures will gain in popularity as more people in the UK try them out.

Prancer

PLATE M

Manufacturer   Arbogast, USA

Classification   Stickbait

Construction   Wooden construction with through-the-body wiring harness. Technically a stickbait, but a really outsized one.

Colours/finish   Six good colours (the same as for the Dasher), including our favourite, Perch Glitter.

Sizes   Comes in three sizes, from 152mm long, 28g to 178mm long, 63g.

Use   Originally designed for sea angling, and already a well-known bass killer on the other side of the Channel, the Prancer fished walking-the-dog style might well pick up an outsize pike. A good surface lure for long casting; the splash should wake something up on a quiet day! An interesting proposition, not for the faint-hearted.

Snooker 7

PLATE I

Manufacturer   Mirrolure, USA

Classification   Stickbait

Construction   Lipless plug; large natural-looking eyes and gills, three trebles; reflective finish.

Colours/finish   Thirty-seven colours – particularly good on natural golds and silvers – plus some vivid options such as Fire Tiger.

Sizes   One size: 92mm long, 10.5g weight.

Use   Very popular in the US for game fishing, the Snooker 7 has an excellent darting action when fished using a twitching motion of the rod tip. Retrieved steadily, it will dive to around 6in and swim like a shallow diver. The usual high-quality Mirrolure finish will stand up to a lot of toothy abuse.

Soft Classic Zara Puppy

PLATE M

Manufacturer   Soft Classic (USA)

Classification   Jerkbait

Construction   Made from soft plastic of 'wine gum' consistency, the lipless cigar shape is very similar to its namesake, the Zara Puppy. Comes in packs of three, one of which is rigged with a Heddon Excalibur offset hook; there is a special groove in the side of the lure which allows accurate and easy hook positioning.

Colours/finish   Five colours, from virtually transparent Silver Shad to very dark green June Bug, all with glittery flecks.

Sizes   One size: 75mm long, 10g weight.

Use   A weedless, slow-sinking lure which is fished walking-the-dog style, creating a natural darting and weaving fish movement, either on or just below the surface. It casts a mile, is very easy to fish, and can be used in very weedy conditions. A good sweep of the rod is needed to set the hook, the point of which is actually buried inside the lure's plastic body. A very unfamiliar style of lure for UK anglers, both in its construction and the construction material. Don't be put off, however, it's fun to use and it works. Relatively cheap, but not indestructible.

Others to try   Zara Puppy (Heddon, USA).

Thriller
PLATE M

Manufacturer   Suick, USA

Classification   Floating/diving jerkbait

Construction   Thin, flat profile with under-cut jaw and adjustable metal rear-tail fin which changes the diving angle. Painted eyes. Two treble hooks.

Colours/finish   Seventeen colours, from naturals to ultra bright fluorescents.

Sizes   Four sizes: from 114m long, 9g weight to an impressive 255mm, 63g weight version (plus two in sinking format). The 114mm Thriller is made of plastic, the rest are made of wood.

Use   The Thriller is a floating lure which is made to dive by fishing with a series of fast, ripping motions. Primarily designed as a Mus-kie lure, the 7in wooden model is probably the best for UK pike fishing. The Thriller's action is very reminiscent of a distressed jack pike. Weighted models plus some customized weighted models are also available. This lure is a household name amongst the muskie men in the US, where it was once nearly banned on one water for being too good a catcher! Highly rated by big fish anglers, but not for the abso-lute beginner.

Top 45
PLATE M

Manufacturer   Yo-Zuri, Japan

Classification   Stickbait

Construction   Slim minnow-shaped lipless plug with moulded gills, eye and scales. Two Mustad trebles attached with split rings, one at the head and one at the belly. The attach-ment point is, unusually, at the tail.

Colours/finish   Comes in two metallic colours, gold and blue.

Sizes   Available in one size only: 80mm long, 5g weight.

Use   A dainty little lure to be twitched on the surface, imitating a feeding baitfish. Designed for perch, trout and pike, it works best in the early part of the season. The hooks are a rather garish gold colour, and you might want to change these for something more restrained.

Ugly Albert
PLATE M

Manufacturer   Gaines Phillips, USA

Classification   Stickbait

Construction   Shaped like a fat cigar, painted eye, two size-2 trebles.

Colours/finish   A good choice of 24 colours range from transparent to black, including nine which have a faint luminous glow.

Sizes   One size: 102mm long, 21g weight.

Use   This floating bait rests upright in the water, with its nose sticking out. Fish it in short jerks, walking-the-dog style, for a dart-ing, skittering motion which appeals to early and late season pike. Strikes will often come within an instant of the first twitch of the lure. The usual very strong Gaines Phillips construction.

Woodwalker
PLATE M

Manufacturer   Luhr-Jensen, USA

Classification   Stickbait

Construction Made from cured sugar pine, this lure has a slightly bulbous cutaway head and curvy body, large carved and painted eyes, two trebles.

Colours/finish Fourteen bright colours (Rainbow Trout is a favourite) with a very high quality finish.

Sizes Three sizes: 53mm long, 10.5g weight; 80mm long, 14g weight, 104mm long, 17.5g weight.

Use A very responsive stickbait, easy to fish, the Woodwalker has been around for years. The current version has been re-designed by US specialist Charlie Campbell (its full name now being the Ozark Charlie Campbell Woodwalker). Seems to fish best when the surface is very calm – its action may be a bit too quiet for the fish to notice it in rougher conditions. A great lure on its day.

Zara Gossa   *PLATE M*

Manufacturer Heddon, USA

Classification Sinking stickbait

Construction Jointed slow-sinking lure with an unusual 'flat back' design and triangular cross-section. Two extremely sharp trebles attached with split rings.

Colours/finish Eight colours, including three G-Fleck finishes.

Sizes Currently one size only 127mm long, 11g weight, but watch out for a baby version and possibly soon, a magnum version.

Use This lure is best fished in walking-the-dog style, when it will move erratically up and down, left and right and even backwards, giving a very lifelike impression of a fish in

trouble. Enjoyable and easy to fish, it is so new that it doesn't have a UK track record – but it will undoubtedly be popular with stickbait fans. A very interesting addition to the famous Heddon range.

Others to try This new lure is designed to fish in the way that soft baits (so very popular in the US) do. No real alternative in hard baits.

Zara Spook   *PLATE M*

Manufacturer Heddon, USA

Classification Stickbait

Construction The classic cigar-shaped stickbait, lipless, with two trebles. Once made of wood but sadly, like many old favourites, made out of plastic these days.

Colours/finish Available in Heddon's usual dazzling display of finishes. There are 19 standard finishes, ranging from Yellow Shore Minnow to Perch, Bullfrog and Red-head, as well as six iridescent G-Finishes and the latest addition: the G-Fleck glittery finishes in Rainbow and Blue Shore Minnow.

Sizes Three sizes: Zara Spook: 114mm long, 21g weight; Zara Puppy: 76mm long, 7g weight; and Zara Pooch: 50mm long, 3.5g weight.

Use Launched in 1922 as the Zaragossa Minnow, the Zara Spook was given its present name in 1939. It is the walking-the-dog lure *par excellence*. The technique – a rhythmic twitching motion of the rod tip, retrieving line in between each rod movement – takes a bit of practice, and a light, stiff rod is needed to get the best results. The resulting action of the Zara Spook is well worth the effort. Characterized by the absence of a diving vane which, coupled with its weighting, produces the random dashes of the lure from side to side (and even backwards!) on retrieve.

Others to try **Finger Mullet** (Bagley, USA).

Slapstick (Bill Lewis, USA).
Tall Walker (Bagley, USA).
Ugly Albert (Gaines Phillips, USA).

CHAPTER FIVE
FLOATING DIVERS

This category has by far the largest population of lures. Floating divers are lures which, upon casting, float on the surface, but which, on retrieve, dive below the surface to greater or lesser depths.

The term 'floating divers' covers several types of lures, and the numerous subdivisions can be a bit confusing. Perhaps the biggest group consists of the minnows. These are slim, roughly fish-shaped lures, frequently made of balsa wood, which produce a fish-like, tight action. They are designed to imitate the predator's food fish, and are very good in clear water or when fish are shy. A good example of this kind of lure is the Rapala Minnow.

Another large group of floating divers are the so-called alphabet lures. These familiar plugs are fat, normally very buoyant lures, which have a wider, more exaggerated wiggle than the minnow group. Diving performance is controlled by the diving vane. (They often have a rattle which adds to their attraction.)

The most famous alphabet lure is the Big S from Shakespeare, although the original lures from which the Big S derives are the Big O (Cordell) and Big N (Bill Norman). The shallow diving versions are deadly in shallow, weedy water in summer, and can be cast long distances. The deeper divers provide a useful change of action in deeper water.

Another lure which you will encounter is the banana lure. Banana lures are, as the name suggest, curved like a banana. Luhr-Jensen's Kwikfish is probably one of the best known examples. They tend to have a wide, shaking side-to-side movement, which creates tremendous vibration in the water. This can easily be felt, as it is transmitted up the rod during the retrieve. The banana lures are at their best being trolled. They can be used from the bank, but tend not to cast particularly well. (Banana lures also come in sinking versions, for example the Canadian Wiggler.)

You will also come across the crankbait. This term originates from the winding or cranking motion you make with the reel handle when working your lure down to its depth. It is rather a vague term, and it's hard to find a definition with which everyone agrees, so we have tended not to use it. However, if you come across it, it's fairly safe to assume that the writer means 'a floating diver which isn't a minnow'.

The depth to which a floating diver will dive is mainly determined by the angle and size of the diving vane, and they all have a maximum depth below which they will not go (unless, of course, you use a downrigger!). Heddon's Hellcat, for example, will dive 2–3ft, but it will not dive to 12ft however hard you try! You can of course weight it down, in which case it will sink to any depth you let it, but in effect you will have created a new lure with a new action.

Many lures have their diving depths printed on their packaging, but quite a few don't, especially the cheaper ones which come from the Far East. When you look at a lure, you can judge whether it's likely to be a shallow, medium or deep diver by looking at the diving vane. As a rough guide, check out the size and angle of the diving vane or lip. Deep divers tend to have big shallow lips, and shallow divers have smaller lips, almost at right angles to the body. Once you've established the diving depth of a lure, if you're forgetful, you can write it on the body of the lure with an indelible marker pen. This will save you a bit of trial and error on the bank, which can eat into valuable fishing time.

Other factors regulating depth are the position of the rod tip and the thickness of the line being used. To achieve maximum depth, the rod tip should point down towards the lure; holding it up will immediately bring the lure up in the water. Thickness of line matters because a thicker line creates more water resistance, and therefore inhibits diving capability. Bear it in mind when choosing your lure fishing line, looking for the best combination of breaking strain and diameter.

A general word on diving vanes and attachment eyes. Both of these affect the depth and the straight running of a lure. If the lure does not run true (i.e. travels to one side or another instead of in a straight line back towards you on the retrieve), bending the attachment eye a *fraction* with a pair of pliers will usually correct this. Some lures are tank-tuned by the manufacturer, and will run absolutely true out of the box; others will need to be tuned when you first use them. Lures can also go out of tune in use, particularly if they've been involved in some hard fights, so always keep an eye out for this.

In the US, the professional bass anglers sometimes deliberately bend the attachment eye so that the lure will swim back at an angle. In this way a bay, corner or an area under an over-hang can be explored more thoroughly. Again, if the eye is moved up or down *fractionally*, the plug will tend to swim a little differently – the effect depending on the design of the lure.

Metal vanes can be adjusted to change running depth (up for deeper, down for shallower), but there is a risk that you'll never get it back to the way it was, so it's not usually a good idea. Don't be tempted to try and alter

a lure's performance by shaving the plastic vane; this almost always ends in disappointment.

———— ♦ ————

Arbogaster PLATE G

Manufacturer   Arbogast, USA

Classification   Floating diver

Construction   Dumpy-bodied, with a large, squarish metal lip. Two treble hooks; the tail hook is dressed with a natural rubber skirt. A rattling version is also available.

Colours/finish   The usual splendid Arbogast colour range, from Black (good for night work) through Tennessee Shad and Perch to Yellow Shore Minnow. A range of glittery 'Flash' finishes is a recent introduction. All Arbogasters have contrasting-coloured rubber skirts.

Sizes   Two sizes: 57mm long, 7g weight; 70mm long, 18g weight.

Use   A deep diver (10–15ft), the Arbogaster gets down surprisingly deep for such a small lure. First produced in 1956, this is another lure which has stood the test of time – a couple of generations of anglers have proved its worth. The metal diving vane makes it suitable for fishing over rocky bottoms, and it's stable when trolling. It will also work as a shallow runner, using a very slow retrieve. A good, deep-water lure for casting or trolling, suitable for pike, perch, loch trout, ferox and salmon.

Arc Minnow
PLATE H

Manufacturer   Yo-Zuri, Japan

Classification   Floating diver

Construction   Plastic-moulded, with a good light-reflecting finish. Distinctive slightly hollowed belly and sharp nose. Inset plastic diving vane; two trebles attached with split rings.

Colours/finish   Four good colours, grey, gold, blue and orange.

Sizes   Three sizes: 90mm long, 6.5 weight; 110mm long, 11g weight; 130mm long, 19g weight.

Use   The Arc Minnow is constructed so as to have a Starlite or Betalite fitted. *Don't!* Under present law, the use of lights as part of a lure is illegal (apparently because they are devastatingly effective in attracting salmon, to the detriment of stocks and fair sport). The alternative use of a filter pad impregnated with an attractant is both legal and a good idea. Use with the added attractor in badly coloured water or when the fish are being difficult. Very popular for pike.

Baby Bopper
PLATE K

Manufacturer   Hokev, Hungary

Classification   Floating diver

Construction   Moulded-plastic alphabet plug, with a slightly humped back. Moulded-plastic lip; two trebles attached with split rings.

Colours/finish   Five colours, our favourite being the bright yellow Tiger.

Sizes   Available in one size only: 70mm long, 10g weight.

Use   A small, medium-diving (to 4ft) plug, good for small water work, suitable for perch and pike. A good value lure for the beginner.

Baby N
PLATE K

Manufacturer   Bill Norman, USA

Classification   Floating diver

Construction   Typical alphabet shape, with integral squarish lip, painted eyes and two trebles attached with split rings.

Colours/finish   Superb range of 57 colours. The prism finishes are particularly good, as are the naturals such as Smokey Joe Shad and Tennessee Shad. Look out, too, for the interesting new glittery sunshine gel coats.

Sizes   Available in one size only: 51mm long, 7g weight.

Use   The Baby N is very characteristic of this group of plugs, and is a good choice for small water, mid-season fishing. Runs from 2–6ft, but watch out for your speed of retrieve – go too fast and it will flip in the water and lose all action.

Baby Pike Getim
PLATE J

Manufacturer   Shakespeare, UK

Classification   Floating diver

Construction   Imitation pike fry, with moulded gills and eyes, two trebles (a bit on the small side), screw fittings and unusual square-shaped opaque plastic diving vane.

Colours/finish   One colour, gold and green pike.

Sizes   One size: 95mm long, 12g weight.

Use   At rest, this lure suspends in the water upright, floated by the large plastic lip. This shallow diver has a rolling wiggle which, coupled with the fry shape, should attract pike. This newly introduced lure will prove popular with Shakespeare fans, offering something a bit different.

Others to try   **Little Jack** (Corado, Poland).

Baitfish   *PLATE I*

Manufacturer   Lindy Little Joe, USA

Classification   Floating diver

Construction   Made from high-impact closed-cell plastic foam, with a stainless steel insert through its body, going from the lip to the hook eyelets. Conventional minnow shape with prominent eyes and an unusual large, squarish, integral diving bill. Two trebles (three on the largest size) attached with split rings.

Colours/finish   Twenty-one colours, mainly bright, strong on yellows and reds. Tennessee Shad and Wounded Perch look particularly useful for UK waters.

Sizes   Three versions: the largest is 152mm long and dives to 25ft, and there are two 108mm long versions: a shallow diver to 4ft and a deep diver to 14ft.

Use   A very strong plug designed for durability, guaranteed not to chip, crack, splinter or absorb water. Not surprising when you consider that this lure is aimed at catching some of the toughest fish around: lake trout, salmon and steelhead. Baitfish has a natural swimming action; use a medium-speed hesitating retrieve for best results. A good choice for heavy-duty applications.

Balsa B   *PLATE K*

Manufacturer   Bagley, USA

Classification   Floating diver

Construction   Fat alphabet shape, with short squarish lip, painted eyes and two treble hooks attached with split rings.

Colours/finish   Very wide colour range, including rather flashy new sparkle finishes.

Sizes   Three sizes: 50mm long, 12g weight; 60mm long, 16g weight; 76mm long, 18g weight.

Use   This is a shallow-water lure, particularly favoured for use on summer still waters with surface-growing weed. Superbly finished, the balsa wood construction gives super buoyancy and a big wiggle – this is one of the originals in Bagley's well known 'B' line-up. Primarily a pike lure in the UK, it is also used as a surface lure for rock fishing for bass and pollack.

Others to try   **Fat Cat** (Bagley, USA).

Bang-O-B   *PLATE F*

Manufacturer   Bagley, USA

Classification   Floating diver

Construction   Really brawny baitfish-shaped lures made from buoyant hardwood. Very strong transparent lexan lip, large painted eyes and two heavy-duty cadmium hooks attached by split rings.

Colours/finish Top quality high gloss finish, available in 21 colours (plus 11 glitter finishes in the 153mm version).

Sizes Two sizes: 153mm long, 42g weight; 205mm long, 61.5g weight.

Use Specialist trolling lure, very strong and true running up to speeds of 18 knots. Diving to 20ft and 30ft respectively, the lexan lips are resistant to damage from rocky bottoms. Designed for big game fish such as wahoo and grouper, these have also found favour amongst pikers and ferox anglers fishing the big lochs.

Bang-O-Lure   *PLATE F*

Manufacturer Bagley, USA

Classification Floating diver

Construction Classic wooden slim minnow with transparent lexan diving vane and two (in larger versions three) treble hooks attached with split rings. Hardwood spine reinforces a balsa body.

Colours/finish A range of 14 colours (not all colours are available in all sizes). The best-sellers are Hot Tiger and Tennessee Shad.

Sizes Five sizes ranging from 50mm long, 5.25g weight to 178mm long, 24.5g weight.

Use A versatile family of lures, suitable for fresh or seawater use, most working from the surface down to 1½ft, the 7in version diving to 4ft. A very slender body with a classic minnow action, the hardwood spine and quality fittings make the Bang-O-Lure very tough. The hardwood adds weight to the lure, making it easier to cast than the traditional all-balsa minnow, whilst the balsa contributes buoyancy. It's useful to have a family of lures with the same action but in different sizes in your armoury.

Others to try Also available (in some sizes) in deeper-diving and spinner-tail (with a propeller) versions.

Believer   *PLATE H*

Manufacturer Rays Tackle, USA

Classification Floating diver

Construction Made from high-impact moulded resin – hook eyes are moulded into the body for maximum resistance to twisting. A flattened drop head creates the diving vane. One, two or three trebles depending on the size of the plug. Larger sizes have two attachment points enabling the lure to be fished deep or shallow.

Colours/finish Twenty-eight colours, very strong in reds and yellows – some good metallics too.

Sizes Five sizes ranging from 101mm long, 21g weight to 254mm long, 112g weight.

Use Use for casting or trolling. The Believer has a very realistic wounded baitfish action.

Big Bopper   *PLATE K*

Manufacturer Hokev, Hungary

Classification Floating diver

Construction Robustly constructed classic-shaped alphabet plug, with moulded integral diving vane, moulded eyes and two trebles attached with split rings.

Colours/finish   Five colours, the favourites being Crucial Crucian and Red Robin.

Sizes   One size: 89mm long, 20g weight.

Use   General-purpose shallow-diving plug (to around 2ft), with a nice big wiggle. Good for perch and pike. Eastern European lures (and indeed, many other types of tackle) will be seen increasingly over the coming years. Some of them are of very poor quality; but some, like the Boppers, represent good value.

Big Bud   *PLATE F*

Manufacturer   Heddon, USA

Classification   Floating diver

Construction   Can this be serious? The lure is shaped like a Budweiser beer can with a big-eyed fish head, and comes complete with a diving lip and a little tail spoon. Two trebles attached with split rings. Graphics on the body are authentic. Contents missing!

Colours/finish   Also in Coors can livery.

Sizes   One size: 70mm long, 18g weight.

Use   When nothing's working and the fish are all huddled together malevolently at the very furthest end of the water, well out of casting range, that's the time to get out this lure and remind yourself that fishing is fun!

Big Mac   *PLATE G*

Manufacturer   Storm, USA

Classification   Floating diver

Construction   Very tough one-piece moulding, with a long diving bill, thick-walled body and heavy-duty fittings. Tapered tail and three trebles, attached with split rings.

Colours/finish   An enticing colour range, with fluorescent red probably the outstanding performer (fluorescent red is rated very highly by some as a deep-water colour).

Sizes   Three sizes: Big Mac: 178mm long, 35g weight (dives to 25ft); Little Mac: 140mm long, 18g weight (dives 15–20ft); Shallomac: 153mm long, 4g weight (dives to around 10ft).

Use   One of the best diving lures for salt water, also growing in popularity for fresh-water use. A good trolling lure with a stable, consistent action at depth. Big Mac has the reputation of being nearly indestructible.

Big S   *PLATE K*

Manufacturer   Shakespeare, UK

Classification   Floating diver

Construction   Alphabet-style fat plug with an integral lip and prominent moulded eyes. Hooks are attached with split rings – the fittings are not the most robust we've seen. The injection moulding hole near the rear treble needs examination before use.

Colours/finish   Good range of colours, including the well liked Perch, Yellow and Black Stripe and Silvery Scale.

Sizes   Three sizes: Big 'S': 90mm long, 20g weight; Medium 'S': 75mm long, 12g weight; Small 'S': 60mm long, 8g weight.

Use   This famous plug has proved a highly successful catcher for many years; notable catches include the 1992 British record arctic char, ferox trout, and, of course, many big pike. Dives to 6ft, should be fished with an erratic retrieve at a medium pace to gain maximum effect from its good wobble. Also worth trying fished with the rod tip up, running it slowly just under the surface of the water. Very widely available. Quality-wise, perhaps not the lure it once was.

Bomber Fat A   *PLATE K*

Manufacturer   Bomber, USA

Classification   Floating diver

Construction   Very rounded alphabet-style body with thick inset plastic lip, painted eyes and two treble hooks attached with split rings. Also available in jointed form.

Colours/finish   The A range is available in 30 finishes, including the particularly good-looking Bengal Fire Tiger (in glittery G-Fleck finish) and our favourites, Bass, Perch and Tennessee Shad.

Sizes   Available in five sizes: 32mm long, 4g weight (dives to 5ft); 38mm long, 6g weight (dives 4–6ft); 50mm long, 11g weight (dives 6–8ft); 57mm long, 14g weight (dives 8–10ft); 64mm long, 18g weight (dives 10–14ft).

Use   A very fat lure, ultra buoyant, with a tight action and a strong rattle. One of an excellent family of lures suitable for all freshwater predators. The light and ultra-light versions are very popular small-water lures. No crankbait is weed-proof, so keep clear of the weeds!

Others to try   Big S (Shakespeare, UK).
Bomber Flat A (Bomber, USA) – thinner profile allows longer distance casting – neutral buoyancy.

Bomber Model A (Bomber, USA) – one-piece moulding, integral bill, will dive to 25ft.

Bullcat   *PLATE G*

Manufacturer   Luhr-Jensen, USA

Classification   Floating diver

Construction   Unusual baby catfish-shaped plastic moulding with tiny stubby dorsal fin, long inset lexan diving bill and two treble hooks.

Colours/finish   Four colours – all darkish shades with fish prints, imitating bottom-feeding bullheads. Channel Cat looks good.

Sizes   One size: 80mm long, 12g weight.

Use   A deep diver, something a bit different to ring the changes. Worth a try for pike when they are bottom feeding on gudgeon, bullheads and the like; try diving down to the bottom and jumping the lure along, allowing the lip to kick up mud, thus giving off a feeding-fish signal.

Burmek B1   *PLATE I*

Manufacturer   Uncle Josh, USA

Classification   Floating diver

Construction   Very robust jointed plug, whose gently convex belly curves down to make a diving lip. Wedge-cut face, moulded eyes and a large stepped back, raised dorsal fin. Three extra-strong Mustad trebles attached with split rings.

Colours/finish   Five colours, Chartreuse Blaze, Black Perch, Jack Pike, Blue Sucker and Black Devil.

Sizes   One size: 204mm long, 56g weight.

Use   This unusual and distinctive plug has been around for over 40 years, and has a tremendous record of success, including a famous haul of 42 muskies in 12 days, 17 of which weighed between 25lb and 52lb. A shallow diver designed for muskie and pike, it can be cast or trolled, and has a natural injured-fish swimming action. Fished slowly just under the surface, it looks like a little shark with the fin breaking the water. Use a slow-to-medium steady retrieve; it can be trolled at very slow speeds without losing performance. A very appealing lure with a growing band of UK enthusiasts.

CC Shad   *PLATE F*

Manufacturer   Cordell, USA

Classification   Floating diver

Construction   Small, attractive roach-shaped body. Inset lexan lip – the attachment ring is on the lip in the larger version, and in the smaller version on the lure body. Two treble hooks, attached with split rings. Good integral rattle.

Colours/finish   A small range of natural colours, which includes one of our all-time favourite finishes: Metallized Perch. Most have scale finishes.

Sizes   Two sizes: Wee Shad: 38mm long, 3g weight (dives 2–4ft); CC Shad: 57mm long, 9g weight (dives 6–8ft).

Use   A small lure suitable for all freshwater predators. The CC is said to stand for Constant Control; the tight action simulates a small baitfish. The Wee Shad is suitable for ultra-light spinning and dives between 2 and 4ft on light line. The standard CC Shad dives 6–8ft, and can be used for trolling (up to 20ft on 10lb test), where it's suspected that the target species are feeding on small baitfish. A little lure which dives deceptively deep.

Conqueror   *PLATE J*

Manufacturer   Corado, Poland

Classification   Floating diver

Construction   Solid plastic plug with inset plastic lip (screw attached to the metal lip on 150mm version). Two trebles attached with split rings.

Colours/finish   Twelve colours, including two very good fish prints (Perch and Trout Parr), an excellent Golden Orfe as well as Dace, Golden Tench etc.

Sizes   Three sizes available: 90mm long, 14g weight; 120mm long, 28g weight; 150mm long, 56g weight.

Use   A good quality floating diver. Introduced into the UK in 1991, it has proved successful for loch salmon (in the Golden Tench and Golden Orfe colours), sea species and notably, pike. Very versatile, and preferred by many people to the more expensive, better-known versions of this type of plug. The two smaller versions dive to between 4 and 6ft, the large version to 10–12ft.

Creek Chub Pikie   *PLATE F*

Manufacturer   Creek Chub, USA

Classification   Floating diver

Construction   Plastic plug with raked head, tapered tail and small moulded eye. Stepped metal diving vane; three treble hooks.

Colours/finish   Just seven highly effective colours: Blue Flash, Red & White, Perch, Pikie, Frog, Sparkle and Yellow Spotted.

Sizes   *Minnow version*; two sizes: 108mm long, 21g weight; 146mm long, 42g weight. *Jointed version*; two sizes: 115mm long, 21g weight; 153mm long, 52g weight.

Use   This is one of the best known and most popular plugs in the UK, and holds, as we write, the UK pike record (Roy Lewis, Llandegfed, 46lb 13oz with a large minnow-bodied perch version). A sturdy, well made plug with a deadly action, the Pikie in both its minnow and jointed forms dives from 4–7ft (casting) and up to 11ft (trolling). The jointed Pikie can be fished a little more slowly than the minnow version, and is good for winter work. A classic for pike and perch, it's also useful for salt-water applications – and we even have reports of chub being taken on the Pikie!

Others to try   **Deep Diving Pikie** (Creek Chub, USA), which has an extended lip and dives around 5ft deeper than standard Pikies. **Lucky Strike Wooden Plug** (Lucky Strike, Canada).

Crystal Minnow   *PLATE H*

Manufacturer   Yo-Zuri, Japan

Classification   Floating diver

Construction   Plastic moulding with a typical Yo-Zuri internally reflecting prism-style body. Two trebles.

Colours/finish   Four colours; orange, blue, gold and metallic grey.

Sizes   Three sizes: 7g, 11g, 18g.

Use   A proven, very popular pike lure, also used for light sea work. Nice rolling action.

Damler (aka **Swim Whiz**)   *PLATE H*

Manufacturer   D.A.M., UK

Classification   Floating diver

Construction   A strongly made lure with a distinctive drop-headed minnow shape with a fat belly, a flattened tail and moulded eyes. Larger sizes have two attachment points on the lip, smaller sizes sport the conventional single point. Treble hooks are attached with split rings – smaller sizes have one or two hooks, larger sizes have three.

Colours/finish   Nine colours are available in the UK, mainly yellow-based with scale finishes on various colours.

Sizes   Five sizes are available: 70mm long, 4g weight (1 treble); 105mm long, 10g weight (2 trebles); 150mm long, 30g weight (3 trebles); 200mm long, 58g weight (3 trebles); 195mm long, 52g weight (jointed, 3 trebles).

Use   This lure, originally made by Northwood Tackle in the US, is now distributed in the UK by D.A.M. under the name Damler. A floating, shallow diver (to around 5ft), it has a very slow, lazy, tail-wagging action, and should be fished slowly with occasional twitches. Very popular for pike.

Others to try   **The Believer** (Rays Tackle, USA).

Dapper Dan   *PLATE J*

Manufacturer   Shakespeare, UK

Classification   Floating diver

Construction   A plastic floating diver with a 'pike'-shaped snout and front-facing painted eyes. Two trebles, the tail treble attached with a screw fitting, the belly treble secured with a metal plate. Curved metal diving vane.

Colours/finish   A range of attractive colours, including a very good green and gold scale.

Sizes   One size: 65mm long, 9g weight.

Use   This popular design was reintroduced by Shakespeare in 1993, and is very similar to the discontinued Heddon River Runt. Its small size makes it a useful alternative to try when the fish seem a bit shy. A shallow diver, it needs to be retrieved at a medium speed to achieve the right action – too fast or too slow will kill it dead. Liked by pike and perch.

Others to try   Also available in a jointed version (**Deeper Dan**; 80mm, 12g) which can be fished a bit slower, and as the name suggests, deeper.

Darter   *PLATE F*

Manufacturer   Creek Chub, USA

Classification   Floating diver

Construction   Plastic floating diver with a wedge-cut lip. Three trebles.

Colours/finish   Five colours. The best is probably Yellow Spotted.

Sizes   Three sizes: 42mm long, 3.5g weight; 57mm long, 7g weight; 96mm long, 14g weight.

Use   This very buoyant minnow-type lure will dive to 6in, making it perfect for running over high-growing weed. Classified here as a floating diver, it could arguably be called a jerkbait. Twitch it using the tip of your rod, and it will dart just like a dying fish. Attractive to all freshwater predators, this is an old standard which in our opinion should be used more often.

Deep Baby N   *PLATE K*

Manufacturer   Bill Norman, USA

Classification   Floating diver

Construction   Typical alphabet body with large, thick integral diving vane. Attachment ring on diving vane and two trebles attached with split rings.

Colours/finish   A range of 57 colours with something to please everyone. Good quality high-gloss finish.

Sizes   One size: 51mm long, 7g weight.

Use   A very fast deep diver, which goes almost straight down to 10ft. Fish it slowly when the desired depth is reached, and you can keep the plug down quite well. It rises very slowly when the retrieve is stopped. A versatile lure for days when a small bait is needed.

Devon Minnow   *PLATE J*

Manufacturer   Gordon Griffiths, UK

Classification   Floating diver

Construction   A minnow body spinning around a hollow central shaft through which is threaded a heavy-duty steel trace. The hook is at the end of this wire. The body has a round cross-section and spins via built-in vanes at 'shoulder' level. Large painted eyes on the top of the head. Also available in sinking versions.

Colours/finish Twelve colours, including all the classic versions plus some less familiar fluorescents.

Sizes Five sizes: 38mm, 51mm, 64mm, 76mm and 102mm.

Use Probably *the* classic lure for salmon and sea trout. At their best in high-water conditions, the Devon Minnow has been a mainstay of game anglers for many years. Yellow Belly (green/yellow) is the traditional favourite, also Blue/Silver. Many brands of the Devon Minnow are available, all conforming to the same design. They are often used in conjunction with the Oval Sprat (see p. 60).

Others to try **Phantail Minnows, Irish Minnows, Crystal Minnow, Quill Minnows** (all from Gordon Griffiths, UK).

Dimpstar   *PLATE H*

Manufacturer Yo-Zuri, Japan

Classification Floating diver

Construction One-piece plastic moulding, with an internal dimple giving a prismatic effect. Inset plastic lip, large eyes, two trebles attached with split rings.

Colours/finish Three colours available; Gold/Clear, Blue/Clear, Black/Clear.

Sizes Two sizes: 110mm long, 12g weight; 130mm long, 18g weight.

Use This shallow-diving lure is a good choice for bass and pollack off the rocks. Its attractive finish will collect light and sparkle in very clear water, making it ideal for those

species which chiefly hunt by sight. Said to be good for zander.

Diving Killer B2 Dredge   *PLATE K*

Manufacturer Bagley, USA

Classification Floating diver

Construction Fat, alphabet shape with elongated tail, large inset plastic lip, painted eyes and two trebles with split rings.

Colours/finish Available in Bagley's excellent colour range, including the new (as we write) sparkle finishes.

Sizes One size only: 64mm long, 18g weight.

Use The deep-diving 'big brother' of the classic B series, with the exaggerated wiggle of the family. This is a slow-sinking lure (1ft per second) which will dive down to 20ft-plus without difficulty. Best fished countdown-style, close to the bottom. A deep-water lure suitable for all freshwater predators.

Others to try **DB3** (Bagley, USA). **DB3 Long Cast** (Bagley, USA).

Equalizer   *PLATE I*

Manufacturer Magna Strike, USA

Classification Floating diver

Construction Plastic plug with flat head and integral lip, tapered tail, big moulded eyes and two treble hooks attached with split rings.

Colours/finish Twenty-five colours ranging from black to white. Chrome-based

'Vibra-Life' finishes are designed for high visibility. The perch variations are amongst the most popular.

Sizes   Three sizes: 165mm long, 56g weight; 133mm long, 28g weight; 102mm long, 14g weight.

Use   This is a very versatile lure which can be used for both casting or trolling in either fresh or saltwater. It has a very tight side-to-side rolling movement, which has proved very popular and successful amongst pike anglers. In the US it is more frequently used for surf casting – when fished slowly, it will run just under the surface, while a speeded-up retrieve will take it down to 10ft. Magna Strike lures are fast gaining in popularity, particularly amongst some of the UK's top lure specialists.

Fat Rap   *PLATE K*

Manufacturer   Rapala, Finland

Classification   Floating diver

Construction   Balsa-bodied 'fat' alphabet-type lure. Inset diving vane with two treble hooks.

Colours/finish   Six colours: Chrome, Bream, Shad, Chrome Blue, Orange, Fire Tiger.

Sizes   Three sizes: Fat Rap: 50mm, 9g (dives 12–14ft); Rattlin' Fat Rap: 70mm, 14g (dives 15–17ft); Mini Fat Rap: 30mm, 4g (dives 4–5ft).

Use   These very buoyant lures will dive well and start to rise in the water during pauses in the retrieve. This makes them suitable for fishing over submerged weeds and above snaggy bottoms. A good versatile lure, suit-

able for pike and, in smaller sizes, for chub and perch.

Fingerling   *PLATE G*

Manufacturer   Luhr-Jensen, USA

Classification   Floating diver

Construction   Natural fish-shaped plug with bulging fry eyes. Large inset plastic diving vane, two trebles attached with split rings.

Colours/finish   Sixteen colours, mainly natural fish prints over foil finishes. Metallic Perch and Shad are particularly attractive.

Sizes   Two sizes: 100mm long, 9g weight; 155mm long, 28g weight.

Use   A deep-diving lure (it will go down as far as 30ft) which can be cast or trolled. Very strongly constructed, this is a popular Great Lakes lure, where it's used for toothy game fish, muskie and northern pike. A quality plug suitable for deep reservoirs and lochs.

Flash Dancer   *PLATE K*

Manufacturer   Arbogast, USA

Classification   Floating diver

Construction   A wide-bodied crankbait, constructed from wood, with a high-quality polyurethane finish. 'Teddy bear' eyes, two trebles attached with split rings.

Colours/finish   A wide range of colours, including some dazzling new glitter effects. (Will they dazzle the fish?)

48

Sizes Available in three sizes: 65mm long with 25g, 18g and 11g weight.

Use Suitable for casting or trolling, across the range of sizes, Flash Dancer dives from 3ft to a claimed 20ft. A newly introduced lure by Arbogast, it is relatively untried in the UK. However, Arbogast is a good stable of lures which includes some real classics, so this is certainly worth consideration.

Gladiator   *PLATE I*

Manufacturer Magna Strike, USA

Classification Floating diver

Construction Slab-sided thin-profiled plug with an inset plastic lip and moulded eyes. Three trebles attached with split rings; freshwater and saltwater hardware alternatives available.

Colours/finish Thirty colours available with a good mixture of natural, metallic, prismatic and bright finishes.

Sizes Two sizes available: 153mm long, 28g weight; 229mm long, 84g weight.

Use This lure was previously known as the Grandma Enticer, and under that name built up an excellent reputation amongst pike anglers. Its very violent action is quite distinctive, and provokes savage attacks. It can be fished slowly just under the surface, or faster to dive to 6ft. The large version is most suitable for saltwater.

Others to try A new jointed version is being developed as we write, and should be worth a try.

Harrier (aka **Deep Diver No.1**)   *PLATE K*

Manufacturer Gordon Griffiths, UK

Classification Floating diver

Construction Medium-sized plastic-moulded lure. Thick inset plastic diving vane with ring attachment on mid lip. Two treble hooks attached with split rings, rattle.

Colours/finish Eleven colours, perch and green/yellow are particularly popular.

Sizes One size: 76mm long, 12g weight.

Use Versatile medium diver to around 6ft, Harrier rises slowly in the water, making it very good for a sink-and-draw style method. A good all-rounder, widely available.

Hawg Boss Water Dog   *PLATE I*

Manufacturer Worden Yakima, USA

Classification Floating diver

Construction Fish-shaped lure with large, thick, inset transparent diving vane. Very prominent 'teddy bear' eyes and two trebles attached with split rings. The unusual feature of this lure is a pair of stiff plastic filament 'wings', which are attached to the belly hook anchoring point and can be folded out at any desired angle from the body.

Colours/finish One colour; Black/Yellow/White.

Sizes One size: 112mm long, 14g weight.

Use A floating diver (to 6ft), with strange wings which create a lot of bubble and vibration. Even without the wings, this is a good-looking lure, and worth trying if you think your local fish are wise to everything you've been throwing at them. Experiment with adjusting the wing position – we haven't reached any conclusion on what works best.

Hellbender (aka Magnum Hellbender)
PLATE F

Manufacturer Heddon, USA (Originally Whopper Stopper Inc)

Classification Floating diver

Construction Big-headed plug with a distinctive heart-shaped lip, two treble hooks and a tail spoon attached with a swivel.

Colours/finish Available in a good range of 16 colours, including an excellent black-and-white G-Finish; the fluorescent green-based colours are useful for the fading light of the deep water of lochs and reservoirs.

Sizes Now only available in Magnum version: 140mm long, 25g weight – always the most popular size.

Use A very deep diver (to 35ft) with a big wiggle, excellent for deep pits and lochs. The tough lip enables it to flip over obstacles, and the little tail spoon adds extra flash to the performance. It's such a good diver, the Americans sell a hookless version designed to tow shallower diving lures down to the depths – a sort of poor man's downrigger!

Hellcat
PLATE F

Manufacturer Heddon, USA (originally Whopper Stopper Inc)

Classification Floating diver

Construction Very slim pointed nosed minnow, with an inset plastic lip and three trebles attached with split rings.

Colours/finish Nine colours – the vivid Fire Tiger is particularly popular, though we prefer the more natural Bass.

Sizes Available in one size only: 115mm long, 10g (the Magnum Hellcat is no longer made).

Use As this is a pretty light lure, its size and shape make it quite difficult to cast a distance, but it is still a useful plug with a lifelike wiggling action. The Hellbender will dive to around 2ft if worked hard. Can also be used for trolling, or fished deep with an added weight. Some feel that three hooks are unnecessary, but remember to make an adjustment in the lure's weight and balance if you remove one of them.

Hi-Lo
PLATE J

Manufacturer Abu Garcia, UK

Classification Floating diver

Construction The Hi-Lo's adjustable metal diving vane gives a diving performance ranging from virtually a surface chugger (when the lip is set almost at a right angle), to a medium diver. Available in floating, sinking and jointed forms.

Colours/finish Available in nine colour schemes, Bright Blue/Silver, Frog and Flame Orange/Black being particularly striking.

Sizes Sinking version: 12g, 18g; jointed version: 20g; floating version: 26g, 40g.

Use The original adjustable lip makes this a very versatile river and lake lure, ideal for the roving lure angler. A very well proven design, which has been around for years.

Others to try **Hi-Lo Minnow** (Abu Garcia, UK) – has a similar action with a conventional minnow body.

Hot Lips Express *PLATE G*

Manufacturer Luhr-Jensen, USA

Classification Floating diver

Construction Nicely moulded fat fish-shaped body with a strange tri-lobed lexan diving lip (hence the name). Painted eyes, two sensible-sized VMC hooks.

Colours/finish A wide range of choice from 22 colours; Fire Red and Fire Tiger are liked for this deep worker.

Sizes Three sizes: 55mm long, 7g weight; 70mm long, 14g weight; 85mm long, 21g weight.

Use A small lure which dives very deeply for its size (to 18ft). Most useful if your target fish are feeding on small baitfish at depth, and you want to copy their size and general shape. The big lip pulls this lure down quickly, and the plug has a nice wiggle. An excellent option when trolling, too.

Hot Shot *PLATE K*

Manufacturer Luhr-Jensen, USA

Classification Floating diver

Construction Fat-bodied plug with a long raking bill and tail fins. One (two on larger sizes) treble hook attached with a split ring. Three sizes are available with a rattle.

Colours/finish Some 45 colours, including a specialist trout range. Something for every application here, but not all sizes are available in all colours.

Sizes Seven sizes, from a tiny 38mm long, 2.5g weight to the 82mm long, 18.5g version.

Use The smaller sizes are designed for trout trolling, the larger sizes can be cast or trolled. The very largest size dives to 18ft and holds the IGFA line class Steelhead record at 30lb 5oz. The Hot Shot swims upright in the water and has a fast, intense wobble; it's a versatile lure, and though it was designed primarily as a trout lure, perch and pike will also take an interest.

Hunter (aka **Deep Diver 2**)
PLATE K

Manufacturer Gordon Griffiths, UK

Classification Floating diver

Construction This lure has a huge integral lip, the characteristic of the real deep diver. The attachment ring is part-way down the lip.

Colours/finish Available in six natural colours. Perch and Bream are very well liked.

Sizes One size: 95mm long, 18g weight.

Use The Hunter is one of the slimmer deep-diving alphabet-type lures. Use in deep water, where it has gained a reputation of working when nothing else does.

Husky *PLATE H*

Manufacturer Rapala, Finland

Classification Floating diver

Construction A balsa-bodied minnow with three trebles. Its 11g casting weight makes it a good bet where long casting is needed. A jointed version is also available.

Colours/finish Four colours; Silver, Blue, Orange, Perch.

Sizes One size: 130mm, 11g (dives 8–10ft).

Use A fairly standard medium-diving minnow, with marine quality hooks; this is an excellent summer lure for inshore bass.

Indiana Plug
PLATE H

Manufacturer D.A.M., UK

Classification Floating diver

Construction Plastic plug with flat head creating the diving vane, moulded gills and prominent 'teddy bear' eyes. Comes in jointed and double-jointed versions (both have two trebles).

Colours/finish Available in five colours, Orange/Black, Yellow/Black (in these two colours, the plug is known as the Eskimo) Trout, Roach and Perch.

Sizes Available in two sizes: 90mm long, 14g weight (two section); 115mm long, 18g weight (three section).

Use An unusual floating shallow diver, particularly attractive in the three-section version, with a crazy eel-like action. Perhaps not the most robust of lures, but something different to offer the wary pike or perch.

Invincible
PLATE J

Manufacturer Nils Master, Finland

Classification Floating diver

Construction Very strongly constructed balsa-wood plug. Inset diving vane, with the two treble hooks attached with a single section of stainless-steel wire which runs through the entire body. The two largest sizes have three hooks.

Colours/finish A superb range of 58 colours including a good selection of scaley, spotty and striped finishes. The silver-blue version is reported as devastating for salmon.

Sizes Five variants are available: 50mm long, 8g weight (dives to 3ft); 50mm long, 6g weight (dives to 6ft); 120mm long, 24g weight (dives to 6ft); 150mm long, 30g weight (dives to 10ft); 250mm long, 120g weight (dives to 17ft).

Use Offering an undramatic, well balanced side-to-side action, this plug is popular for its strength, true running and its track record for catching pike, trout and salmon. Further afield, the Invincible has proved itself tough enough to catch the likes of barramundi. Experiment with hesitating retrieves, aiming to make the lure look as much like a wounded fish as possible, and results should follow.

Others to try The **Jointed Invincible**, which can be fished a little slower than the standard version.

J-Plug
PLATE G

Manufacturer Luhr-Jensen, USA

Classification Floating diver

Construction A one-piece plastic moulding with the trace channel ready to take the tandem-mounted VMC trebles supplied. The Dacron mounting cord for the trailing hook is probably all right for salmon, but not recommended for pike. A wooden version is also available.

Colours/finish A vast array of colours, from plain silver through to the exotic Chartreuse Fire Dot and Metallic Green Mackerel.

Sizes Four sizes available: 83mm long; 104mm long; 120mm long; and 140mm long.

Use An American version of the Kynoch Killer, an old time salmon lure, the J-Plug shallow dives to around 4–5ft. Its erratic dancing action, not often seen in plugs, makes it a good alternative bait when more conventional plugs have not been performing. Equally good trolled or cast, a reliable general-purpose lure for the bigger predators, pike and salmon.

Javelin
PLATE G

Manufacturer Luhr-Jensen, USA

Classification Floating diver

Construction A heavy-duty minnow, made from lexan high-impact moulded plastic with a moulded-in bill. The cadmium VMC trebles are well anchored with heavy-duty split rings. Its incredibly loud rattle will wake the dead!

Colours/finish Eight colours available.

Sizes One size: 146mm long, 35g weight.

Use A relative newcomer on the lure scene, aimed at the sea angler looking for a good-sized, virtually indestructible lure for heavy-duty use. This minnow-shaped plug dives 6–10ft (casting) and is highly suitable for deep-water pike trolling. Its excellent casting ability makes it ideal, too, for pit and reservoir piking.

Jensen Minnow
PLATE G

Manufacturer Luhr-Jensen, USA

Classification Floating diver

Construction Plastic-moulded flat-bellied minnow with two sensible-sized hooks (not the grappling irons some US lures come equipped with) and a nice big painted eye.

Colours/finish Seventeen colours are listed, Brown Trout and Blue/Silver have particular appeal as attractive fish takers.

Sizes Available in five sizes ranging from 63mm long, 4g weight to 140mm long, 14g weight.

Use A good general-purpose minnow-type lure, aimed at short-range plug fishing. A lighter version of the Javelin, the Jensen Minnow is designed to be fished with a twitching, jerking or ripping action. Suitable for all predators, but doesn't stand up as well as some to very heavy-duty use.

Jointed Floating

Manufacturer Yo-Zuri, Japan

Classification Floating diver

Construction A jointed minnow with an inset plastic diving vane, large 'teddy bear' eyes and two treble hooks attached with split rings.

Colours/finish Five naturalistic colours; Gold and Blue Mackerel look the best.

Sizes Three sizes: 90mm long, 10g weight; 110mm long, 15g weight; 130mm long, 23g weight.

Use Yo-Zuri lures are highly rated by many lure anglers. This is perhaps one of their less exciting offerings. None the less, its smooth minnow action, solid construction and good quality fittings make it worthy of consideration, for freshwater and light sea work.

Others to try Also available in a sinking version.

Killer Plug   *PLATE J*

Manufacturer Gordon Griffiths, UK

Classification Floating diver

Construction Wooden-bodied minnow with a raked-back dish face, tapered tail and a painted eye. A hollow shaft runs from the centre of face diagonally to the belly. The treble hook is attached to a split ring, which is in turn attached to a snap and a swivel, the whole of which is threaded through the shaft. The hook is prevented from going through the shaft by the split ring.

Colours/finish Seven hand-painted colours including traditional Yellow Belly and Blue/Silver.

Sizes Two sizes: 76mm long and 102mm long, 20g weight.

Use This popular traditional lure is mainly used for salmon. The structure of the lure means that the body slides up the line, thus preventing a strong fish from using it as a lever to rid itself of the hook. A very wide tail-wagging action is also attractive to pike. Good casting plugs, also suitable for trolling.

Kwikfish   *PLATE I*

Manufacturer Luhr-Jensen, USA

Classification Floating diver

Construction Plastic-moulded banana-shaped plug with flattened head and blunt tail. Smaller sizes have one (larger sizes two) treble hooks, which are attached with split rings.

Colours/finish Almost 100 colours and finishes, including a special salmon and steelhead range. The all-out favourites are still the plainer metallic finishes, along with frog and coachdog.

Sizes Twelve sizes, ranging from an ultra-lite version (K3: 33mm long and weighing just one gram) to the popular K15 version (125mm long, weighing 30g).

Use A floating diver, the Kwikfish can be used for casting or trolling (though it can only be described as a short-range casting lure, due to its unaerodynamic shape). It has a tremendous vibrating action, which takes a bit of getting used to – it feels rather like a big bunch of weed snagged up on the lure. In the UK, the Kwikfish is regarded by many as *the* lure for perch – and it's the largest size they go for. Should be fished or trolled slowly for maximum effect. Use for perch, pike, trout and salmon.

Others to try **Jointed Kwikfish** (Luhr-Jensen, USA).

Lazy Ike   *PLATE I*

Manufacturer Lazy Ike, USA

Classification Floating diver

Construction Plastic-moulded, hump-backed banana-shaped plug with a long flattened bill and two trebles.

Colours/finish Eight colours (four metallic and four bright), the best known of which is the red head with the rather Egyptian-looking painted eye.

Sizes Four sizes; Magnum Ike: 90mm long, 17.5g long; Mighty Ike: 76mm long, 9.3g weight; Lazy Ike: 57mm long, 7g weight; Mite Ike: 51mm long, 3.5g weight.

Use The key thing to remember about Lazy Ike is its name: it's a really slow, lazy-looking lure, which is only effective when fished very slowly with a nice, steady retrieve. A good trolling lure, it's perfect where slow trolling is wanted. The Ike works at 3–5ft (the Mite Ike) down to 7–9ft (the Magnum Ike) for casting, and from 9–11ft (the Mite Ike) down to 15–17ft (the Magnum Ike) for trolling.

Others to try **Hellin Flat Fish** (Worden Yakima, USA).

Limper Jointed
PLATE I

Manufacturer Shakespeare, UK

Classification Floating diver

Construction Jointed 'banana'-type plug with screw fittings and two trebles. The tail has a notched fin shape, and the tail hook is attached to a wire which goes right through the fin and is, in turn, attached to a screw on the main body. No eyes.

Colours/finish Limited colour range.

Sizes One size: 90mm long, 10g weight.

Use A floating diver with a most attractive erratic snaking action, designed to imitate and injured quarry fish. Best fished slowly with occasional spurts, this could be a good perch catcher. Widely available.

Others to try **Jointed Kwikfish** (Luhr-Jensen, USA).

L-Jack Minnow
PLATE H

Manufacturer Yo-Zuri, Japan

Classification Floating diver

Construction Moulded plastic with clever internal prism giving a 'deep' iridescence. Mustad hooks, but the other fittings don't look as good.

Colours/finish Four colour schemes, all iridescent, orange, blue, gold and rainbow – very attractive.

Sizes Five sizes: from 6g to 45g in both floating and sinking versions. A magnum sinking version with a well moulded diving lip is also available.

Use Despite a slight question mark about the quality of the fittings, there is no doubting these lures' record. They are very good catchers and popular with many top lure anglers. Worth a place in the serious lure angler's box.

Little Jack
PLATE J

Manufacturer Corado, Poland

Classification Floating diver

Construction Pike fry-shaped plug with a transparent diving vane and two treble hooks attached by split rings.

Colours/finish Fish print, natural pike colour (the best pike look-alike we've come across).

Sizes   One size: 87mm long, 14g weight.

Use   This popular floating diver works to 5–6ft, and has an attractive slow wiggle. Fitted with an oversize lip, which tends to brush weed aside, Little Jack is easy to fish in lightly weeded water. A real winner for pike.

Long 'A' *PLATE F*

Manufacturer   Bomber, USA

Classification   Floating diver

Construction   A good, solid lure with a moulded-in diving lip. Some models in the family have three treble hooks, others two. Jointed models are also available.

Colours/finish   Very good selection of colours, from white through to some dark gudgeon-like patterns. Brilliant silver and prism colours also available, plus a selection of iridescent G-Finishes.

Sizes   Five sizes available: 90mm long, 7g weight (shallow diver); 90mm long, 11g weight (dives 10–12ft); 114mm long, 11g weight (dives 2–3ft); 114mm long, 11g weight (dives 3–4ft – Jointed); 114mm long, 14g weight (deep diver).

Use   This is an excellent all-round diving minnow, suitable for all coarse-fish predators, and also for light sea work. Popular with many pike specialists, the Long 'A' comes highly recommended as one of the all-time great lures. A heavy-duty version and a Magnum heavy-duty version are available for big pike and deep-sea game species.

Magna Fat Minnow *PLATE I*

Manufacturer   Magna Strike, USA

Classification   Floating diver

Construction   Lipless, fat-bodied rattling lure, with big fry eyes and a flat-top head. Two heavy-duty trebles attached with split rings.

Colours/finish   Some 25 colours, including a large number of dark versions, and a good selection of 'Vibra-Life' ridged chrome finishes. (Our favourite amongst these is Perch.)

Sizes   One size: 67mm long, 11g weight.

Use   Shallow diving lure, particularly good where you want to fish slowly around holding spots, since the Magna Minnow has almost neutral buoyancy. It will maintain its action, which is produced by its wedge-cut front face, even at very slow retrieve rates.

Others to try   Magna Standard Minnow (larger version).
Magna Lil' Minnow (thinner version).
(Both from Magna Strike, USA.)

Magnum Floating *PLATE H*

Manufacturer   Rapala, Finland

Classification   Floating diver

Construction   Minnow-shaped plug with inset diving lip. Robustly constructed from African Odum wood, with very solid hook anchoring and heavy-duty marine quality trebles.

Colours/finish   Five colours available; the mackerel is particularly interesting.

Sizes   Available in one size: 133mm, 11g (dives 8–10ft).

Use   A very good caster, suitable for situations where you'll be casting into strong wind or using extra heavy line. Can be used as a diver, or twitched across the surface. Popular for trolling in the US.

Others to try   Also available in a sinking version for deeper water.

Maverick   *PLATE J*

Manufacturer   Gudebrod Inc, USA

Classification   Floating diver

Construction   Rugged ABS construction, according to the makers – and they mean it. A *very* solid moulding, with 200lb test wire harnessing the hooks together. The rear hook is mounted under the tail, which is claimed to give better action and a better hook-up rate. Prominent moulded eyes.

Colours/finish   Ten colours offered: not spectacular, but well-tried combinations all the same. Gudebrod also offer an unpainted, unhooked version which you can customize to your own requirements – a good money-saving idea.

Sizes   Available in one size only: 152mm long, 56g weight.

Use   This is used in the UK primarily as a sea lure. However, it would be a good trolling lure for freshwater species in shallowish water, and will cast well also. Maverick is the type of lure one turns to on a very windy day on a large expanse of water, when lesser lures won't go out any distance. A shallow diver (to 1ft), it can be fished almost in a walking-the-dog style, twitching and popping like a top-water lure, though the more conventional use is with a steady retrieve.

Meadow Mouse   *PLATE F*

Manufacturer   Heddon, USA

Classification   Floating diver

Construction   Designed to imitate a water vole, right down to its velour coat and long leathery tail. Inset diving vane, two trebles (no squeak).

Colours/finish   Five colour options; white, black, brown, grey and chartreuse.

Sizes   One size: 66mm long, 21g weight.

Use   An excellent summer lure, not only in weedy areas but also in clearer, wider water. Dives to 2ft, though more usually used on or just under the surface. Particularly recommended when cast parallel to the bank and retrieved along the margins, just where you'd expect to find real waterside mammals. A favourite lure – there are lots of totally bald examples living in famous tackle boxes.

Others to try   Although there are several mouse imitations around – **Mr Mouse** (Blimp's Fishing Tackle, USA); **Bass Rat** (Southern Lure Co, USA) – there is no real substitute for a Meadow Mouse.

Medium Diving Snooker Minnow   *PLATE G*

Manufacturer   Arbogast, USA

Classification   Floating diver

Construction   A wooden minnow plug with slightly indented sides and a flattened top to the head. Long inset plastic diving lip and two Mustad Duratin trebles attached with split rings. High-quality finish, typical of Arbogast lures.

Colours/finish   Fourteen colours including two glitter finishes. Best freshwater options are the Perch and Shad versions; Chartreuse and Blue Scale are good for sea work.

Sizes   Three sizes: 89mm long, 10.5g weight; 114mm long, 14g weight; 140mm long, 21g weight.

Use   A highly buoyant lure which is nonetheless very easy to cast. The sleek minnow shape gives a very smooth swimming action, using a medium-speed retrieve. The hardware is corrosion-resistant, so this lure can be used in salt or fresh-water. Dives very quickly to 5–6ft, and is therefore suitable for relatively small and narrow waters, where it gets down to the fishing zone without too much loss of distance.

Others to try   One of a family of Snooker lures, including a jerkbait, tail prop, twin prop, sinking and shallow diving versions.

Mini Fat Rap   *PLATE K*

Manufacturer   Rapala, UK

Classification   Floating diver

Construction   A miniature version of the well-known Fat Rap with an inset plastic diving vane and one treble.

Colours/finish   Four colours available, Orange, Perch, Shad and Crawfish.

Sizes   Just one size: 30mm long, 4g weight.

Use   A popular little baby lure with the exaggerated wiggle characteristic of the alphabet lure. Specifically designed with perch and trout in mind, small (and sometimes not so small) pike also find it a toothsome morsel.

Others to try   Fat A Ultralite (Bomber, USA).

Minx (aka **Shallow Diver**)   *PLATE K*

Manufacturer   Gordon Griffiths, UK

Classification   Floating diver

Construction   Baby alphabet lure with an integral lip, a slightly convex belly, painted eyes and two trebles attached with split rings.

Colours/finish   Six colours, including some effective metallics.

Sizes   One size: 50mm long, 5g weight.

Use   Shallow diver with a very tight wiggle, best worked with a fast retrieve. Its light weight means that its casting abilities are limited, so choose this one for short-range work. Useful on days when bigger plugs are being ignored; liked by perch and small pike.

Mirrolure Jointed Crankbait   *PLATE I*

Manufacturer   Mirrolure, USA

Classification   Floating diver

Construction   Jointed plug with prominent fish eyes, a metal diving vane and two trebles.

Colours/finish   A range of 36 excellent colours, with a very high-quality finish. Sardine is outstanding.

Sizes   One size: 75mm long, 7g weight.

Use   This lure was first produced over 55 years ago and has proved itself over the years as a good catcher of salmon, trout, sea trout and pike, amongst others. Diving to just 6in, it has a very life-like action and is especially effective where weeds are close to the surface.

Others to try   Also available in smaller, sinking versions – **Original Jointed** (Mirro-lure, USA) – including an excellent miniature ultralight which is popular for trout.

Mugger   *PLATE K*

Manufacturer   Ryobi Masterline Ltd, UK

Classification   Floating diver

Construction   A very unusual lure, with built-in 'Jet-Thru' air chambers allowing water to flow through the lure on the retrieve. Inset plastic lip, two correctly proportioned trebles attached with split rings. A rattle is contained in a chamber which runs from side to side of the lure.

Colours/finish   Three colours: Lightning Silver, Fireball Red and Charlie Brown (brown and orange).

Sizes   One size: 80mm long, 11g weight.

Use   The Mugger dives to 8ft. As it dives, air and water are forced through the lure, creating a stream of bubbles, accompanied by lots of sound and vibration, creating a very interesting target for pike, perch and chub. Dr Barrie Rickards tested this for Ryobi, and recommends a hesitant retrieve when fishing the Mugger at depth.

One Minus   *PLATE K*

Manufacturer   Manns, USA

Classification   Floating diver

Construction   Classic 'Fat' shape, great big rattle, extremely buoyant, big painted eyes, two treble hooks.

Colours/finish   Twenty-five colours, from bright chartreuse through to chrome. Bright red is a big favourite, as well as the versions having a touch of yellow.

Sizes   Two sizes: 65mm long, 7g weight; 83mm long, 16g weight.

Use   This shallow-running alphabet lure is guaranteed by the makers not to run deeper than a foot. One of our favourite lures, the red version is especially good. Obviously suitable for the usual shallow applications, especially over weed, this lure also performs well on big waters such as Ardingly Reservoir in Sussex (where it has a good reputation as a catcher), attracting pike up from the depths to investigate.

Original   *PLATE H*

Manufacturer   Rapala, Finland

Classification   Floating diver

Construction   Thin balsa-bodied minnow. Conventional design, small trebles and very well finished – as are all Rapala lures. Also available in Jointed form.

Colours/finish   Nine colours including Silver, Gold, Blue, Gold/Orange, Rainbow Trout, Yellow/Silver, Fire Tiger and Perch.

Sizes   Minnow: 50mm long, 3g weight (dives 4–5ft), 70mm long, 4g weight (dives 4–6ft); 90mm long, 5g weight (dives 4–6ft); 110mm long, 6g weight (dives 5–7ft); 130mm long, 7g weight (dives 6–8ft); 180mm long, 11g weight (dives 9–11ft).

Use A very lightweight lure, the Original is excellent fished at or close to the surface on a slow retrieve. A faster retrieve will crank the bait down to its working depth. A good all-round lure for most predators (coarse, game and sea), these lures are very subtle and responsive, which accounts for Rapala's popularity over many years on both sides of the Atlantic, and indeed, around the world.

Oval Sprat   *PLATE J*

Manufacturer Gordon Griffiths, UK

Classification Floating diver

Construction Very similar to the Devon Minnow, but with two important differences. First, the body is oval rather than round. Second, by tradition the Oval Sprat rotates in the opposite direction to the Devon Minnow. Since both lures are used in similar situations, the idea originally was to switch to the Sprat after using the Devon, so as to untwist the kinks put in by the Devon! These days, we have high-quality swivels to help us avoid kinks altogether. Also comes in sinking versions.

Colours/finish As for Devon Minnow (see p. 46).

Sizes Three sizes: 64mm long; 76mm long; 89mm long.

Use See Devon Minnow, p. 46.

Others to try Sinking Oval Sprat (Gordon Griffiths, UK).
Strathallan Minnow (Gordon Griffiths, UK).
Original Sprat (Gordon Griffiths, UK).

Phred's Shadeaux   *PLATE G*

Manufacturer Arbogast, USA

Classification Floating diver

Construction A bulky minnow-shaped lure, made of wood with prominent 'teddy bear' eyes, a wide rounded diving vane and two trebles attached with split rings.

Colours/finish Nine colours are available, including glitter finishes.

Sizes Available in two sizes: 70mm long, 11g weight; 89mm long, 14g weight, covering a diving range from 3ft down to 12ft.

Use Phred's Shadeaux is suitable for casting or trolling, and this relative newcomer could well find a place as a bass lure worked off the rocks. Arbogast lures have a very good reputation for both quality and design, and this one could well take its place alongside other classics from the same stable. A recent introduction to the UK market, its Perch, Fire Tiger and Rainbow Trout colours will probably prove to be favourites.

Pike Plug – 3 section   *PLATE H*

Manufacturer D.A.M., UK

Classification Floating diver

Construction Double-jointed minnow-shaped plug with large realistic 'teddy bear' eyes, large inset lip and two heavy-duty trebles attached with split rings. The front joint is attached in two places for additional strength.

Colours/finish One colour: a green, yellow and white pike imitator.

Sizes Four sizes: 90mm long, 10g weight; 110mm long, 16g weight; 130mm long, 25g weight; 150mm long, 40g weight.

Use Three-sectioned plugs are not very common, and this one has a nice snaky movement. Dives fast to around 5ft; the larger size can be used for casting or trolling, and has hooks suitable for sea use. The smaller sizes are a useful addition to the piking armoury.

Others to try **Jointed Thunderstick** (Storm, USA), which also has a good snaky action.

Pike Special *PLATE H*

Manufacturer D.A.M., UK

Classification Floating diver

Construction A very tough plug, wired through, large inset lip, prominent 'teddy bear' eyes and two very large trebles attached with split rings.

Colours/finish One colour: transparent with an encapsulated yellow reflective film.

Sizes Three sizes: 170mm long, 45g weight; 200mm long, 70g weight; 240mm long, 100g weight.

Use A really meaty plug, which, as the name suggests, is designed for pike. However, all but the smallest size would probably be considered too large for most people's taste. But big shallow-diving lures can be very effective, and this one is certainly tough enough for the job. Could be a good one to try for sea species, too.

Others to try **Burmek** (Uncle Josh, USA).

Predator *PLATE I*

Manufacturer Magna Strike, USA

Classification Floating diver

Construction Slightly bulbous body with a tapered tail, flat-topped sloping head with a wedge mouth and large prominent eyes. Two heavy-duty treble hooks attached by split rings. Solidly built.

Colours/finish Twenty-five colours, ranging from black to white, and eight metallic finishes. The Green or Blue Mackerel stand out for sea use, the Perch variations for freshwater. The paint tends to wear off rather quickly.

Sizes Three sizes: 159mm long, 56g weight; 127mm long, 28g weight; 96mm long, 14g weight.

Use With its rolling side-to-side action with a wide tail waggle, this lure can be fished very slowly without losing its action – a valuable attribute, especially in winter. Can be worked from the surface down to 6ft, and effective for beach casting, fishing around rocks, trolling, river and lake fishing – a real all-rounder.

Rattlin' Flat Wart *PLATE G*

Manufacturer Storm, USA

Classification Floating diver

Construction Rounded Wart shape, but with flattened sides. Long integral diving lip, painted eyes, ball-bearing rattle and two treble hooks.

Colours/finish Thirty-two colours ranging over naturals, bright fluorescents and metallics.

Floating Divers

Sizes   One size: 76mm long, 21g weight.

Use   A deeper diver than the well-known Wiggle Wart (10–14ft), with a tighter, narrower action, giving a more natural-looking movement. Fished with a hesitant retrieve, it rises up in the water fairly slowly as you slow down or stop reeling, and will often be struck at this point.

Others to try   The whole **Wiggle Wart** family are worth a look.

Rattlin' Rogue   *PLATE F*

Manufacturer   Smithwick, USA

Classification   Floating diver

Construction   Slimline minnow shape with diving performance from 1–10ft plus in the range. All models are equipped with three trebles except the smallest (RA1200), which has two. All have good rattles. The largest (SSRB1200) is a suspending lure (meaning it has neutral buoyancy and so will hang suspended at the depth to which it's cranked down).

Colours/finish   Twenty-seven colours; gold and silver foil variants are the Smithwick speciality.

Sizes   Five sizes, from 90mm long to 153mm long, weights range from 7g to 10.5g. The diving depth increases up the size scale from a shallow diving 1ft model up to the biggest, which will comfortably reach a depth of 10ft.

Use   This lure has an excellent pedigree in the US Bass circuit. The deeper-diving models are best left for weed-free areas in winter. The neutral buoyancy model is popular for fishing around known underwater holding points, e.g. submerged trees, super-

market trolleys, where it can be held in place and twitched like a surface lure. Also much liked as a deep-water trolling lure.

Rebel Minnow

Manufacturer   Rebel, USA

Classification   Floating diver

Construction   Standard minnow body, inset diving vane, painted eye, two trebles attached with split rings. The larger versions come equipped with corrosion-proof hooks suitable for saltwater use.

Colours/finish   Eleven standard colours, plus six G-Finishes, with mainly natural finishes. A very vivid Fire Tiger is also available.

Sizes   Eleven sizes, ranging from a 38mm long, 2g weight baby ultralite to a brawny 178mm long, 28g weight saltwater model. Most sizes are available in jointed alternatives.

Use   Another very versatile family, suitable for saltwater in the larger sizes. This lure has been around for 30 years, and has been a popular standby throughout that time. It's always useful to have a big family of lures to choose from: you can get used to the action and learn how to use it, and then switch up and down the size range to fit the fishing circumstances you encounter, without having to change your basic lure fishing technique. Diving depths range from 2–4ft. A size is available to suit most target species, from chub up to big sea bass.

Red Fin   *PLATE F*

Manufacturer   Cordell, USA

Classification   Floating diver

Construction   Streamlined minnow shape, with a plastic diving lip (except for the deep-diving Red Fin which has an extra-strong lexan lip). Moulded eyes, two treble hooks attached with split rings (except deep-diving version which has three).

Colours/finish   Some 20 plus colours, including G-Finish (not all models are available in all colours). Gold, chartreuse, copper and silver variations are well represented and are particularly attractive.

Sizes   Red Fin: 102mm long, 11g weight (dives 0–2ft); Jointed Red Fin: 102mm long, 11g weight (dives 0–2ft); Red Fin: 127mm long, 18g weight (dives 0–3ft); Jointed Red Fin: 127mm long, 18g weight (dives 0–3ft); Deep Diving Red Fin: 127mm long, 18g weight (dives 8–10ft); Red Fin: 178mm long, 28g weight (dives 0–2ft).

Use   A good all-purpose shallow diver for saltwater and freshwater alike, well thought of for trout in the US. Jointed versions have very pronounced tail action. Its hollow-head construction gives it a special buoyancy, which makes it very suitable for fishing around snags and for sink-and-draw type working.

Riplin Red Fin   *PLATE F*

Manufacturer   Cotton Cordell, USA

Classification   Floating diver

Construction   Curving fish-shaped lure with wavy sides – hence its name. Inset plastic diving vane, three treble hooks attached with split rings.

Colours/finish   Good range of bright colours. The G-Finish colours are particularly recommended; they are probably the closest copy of natural scale iridescence available.

Sizes   Available in one size only: 114mm long, 21g weight.

Use   Dives 0–3ft. The unusual moulded ripple effect down the length of the body gives a rolling, shivering action. The hollow head gives the Riplin Red Fin an effective fish-like response when twitched; the strong rattle maximizes underwater vibration. Primarily a pike lure in the UK, suitable for shallow weedy lakes, canals and rivers, but also used for spinning off rocks into gullies for bass and pollack. Casts medium range.

Others to try   Red Fin (Cordell, USA).

Shadling   *PLATE L*

Manufacturer   Lindy Little Joe, USA

Classification   Floating diver

Construction   Slim minnow-shaped solid-bodied plug with stainless-steel insert running from the attachment point to the hook eyelets. Long integral diving vane, two treble hooks attached by split rings.

Colours/finish   Twenty-one colours, mostly based on yellow or white bodies, with some attractive metallics.

Sizes   Five versions are available: 76mm long (dives to 6ft); 101mm long (dives to 5ft);114mm long (dives to 10ft); 146mm long (dives to 8ft); 152mm long (dives to 20ft).

Use   Designed for fishing in hard conditions, where fast-running water can easily put a lure out of tune. The stainless-steel insert is designed to ensure that the attachment ring does not get twisted in use. An all-round lure which can be cast or trolled, fish it with a sink-and-draw type retrieve. Suitable for saltwater as well as fresh (though you'll probably want to change the hooks for saltwater use), the Mackerel, Blue Silver Smelt and Chartreuse Silver look particularly good for the sea.

Shad Rap   *PLATE H*

Manufacturer   Rapala, Finland

Classification   Floating diver

Construction   Balsa body with smallish trebles, beautifully finished. Also available in shallow-running form.

Colours/finish   Five colour schemes, with a devastatingly good metallic perch on top of the pile.

Sizes   Deep Runner: 50mm long, 8g weight (dives 6–8ft); 70mm long, 9g weight (dives 8–10ft); 80mm long, 10g weight (dives 10–12ft); 90mm long, 15g weight (dives 12–14ft).

Use   A very well balanced lure, Shad Rap will work true over a wide range of retrieve speeds – a particularly important feature when trolling. Its virtually neutral buoyancy means that pausing in the retrieve will leave the lure hanging suspended in mid-water. Often, this will induce a take. It's a good perch, chub and trout lure, and will also catch pike in the larger sizes.

Shimmy   *PLATE J*

Manufacturer   Gordon Griffiths, UK

Classification   Floating diver

Construction   Plastic-moulded body with a moulded-in lip. Two trebles are attached by screw-in eyes (a touch of strong glue is a good idea). Nice reflective eye.

Colours/finish   Six colours offered; Fire Tiger, a new colour, looks good; Chartreuse and White is very popular.

Sizes   One size: 76mm long, 10g weight.

Use   A medium diver with a slinky, tight wiggle (hence the name), Shimmy is quite widely available. Suitable for pike and perch, trout and salmon, and even for very light sea work.

Short Wart   *PLATE K*

Manufacturer   Storm, USA

Classification   Floating diver

Construction   Small flat plug, wide squarish lip, large moulded eyes, two trebles attached with split rings, ball-bearing rattle.

Colours/finish   A vast range of over 100 colours; the angler is spoilt for choice.

Sizes   One size: 65mm long, 9g weight.

Use   Designed for fishing shallow waters (diving to 4ft) and for deep-water situations, where fish are suspended high up. A quick-diving buoyant lure with a big rattle for its size, Short Wart is fun and reliable, and casts well for its size and weight.

Others to try   Just one of the large **Wiggle Wart** family, ranging from the ultralite **Pee Wee Wart** (Storm, USA) to the deep-diving **Rattlin' Flat Wart** (Storm, USA).

Spearhead   *PLATE J*

Manufacturer   Nils Master, Finland.

Classification   Floating diver

PLATE A

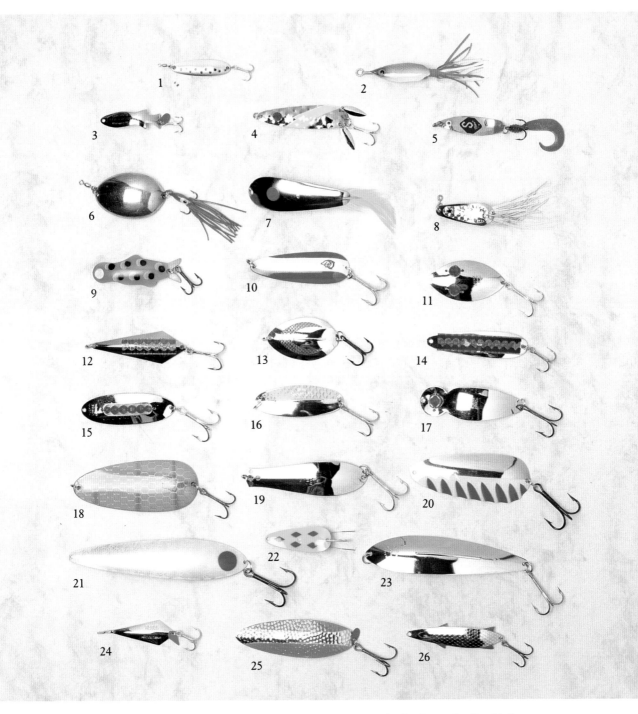

1 Krocodile; 2 Hawaiian Spoon; 3 Banshee; 4 Attractor; 5 Syclops; 6 Squid Spoon; 7 Rex Spoon; 8 Jawbreaker; 9 Cisco; 10 Dardevle; 11 Red Flash; 12 Arrowhead Trolling Spoon; 13 Trophy II; 14 Slammer; 15 Beaded Back; 16 Wabbler; 17 Scarlet Eye; 18 Dardevle Huskie; 19 Doctor Spoon; 20 Half Wave; 21 Canoe; 22 Weedless Devil; 23 Whitefish; 24 Arrowhead Spoon; 25 Lizard; 26 X-2 Rocket.

PLATE B

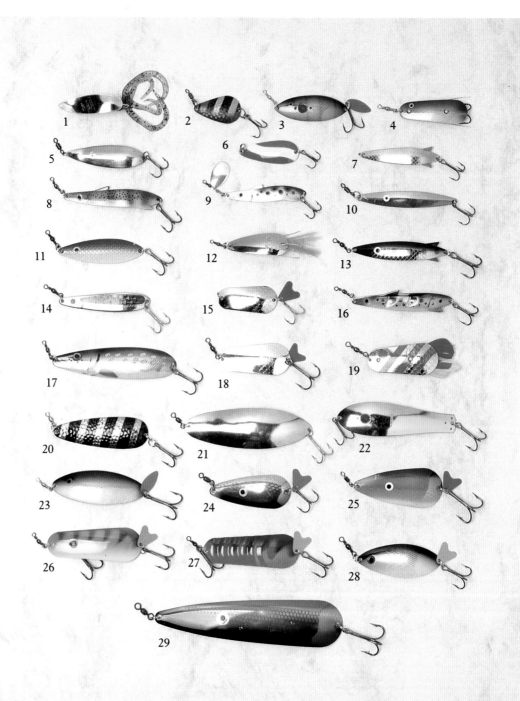

1   Timber Doodle; 2   Ham Spoon; 3   Krokodil; 4   Nix; 5   Kerryman; 6   Devil; 7   Smakk;
8   Lukki; 9   Likki Flip Z; 10   Catcher; 11   Koster; 12   Favourit; 13   Toby; 14   Herri;
15   Tiger; 16   Turbo; 17   Pikko; 18   Kraut; 19   Effzett; 20   Atlantic Spoon; 21   Derrick
Amies Norfolk Spoon; 22   Professor; 23   Turku; 24   Sonic; 25   Miki; 26   Uto; 27   Atom;
28   Stor-Oringen; 29   Heron.

PLATE C

1 Tiger Tail; 2 Switcheroo; 3 Flyer; 4 Droppen; 5 Ultra Spinner; 6 Hawaiian Wiggler;
7 Rooster Tail; 8 Flyer Jig; 9 Lotto; 10 Shyster; 11 Reflex; 12 Bang Tail; 13 Swiss
Lunker; 14 Pygmy Hot'N'Tot; 15 Snagless Sally.

PLATE D

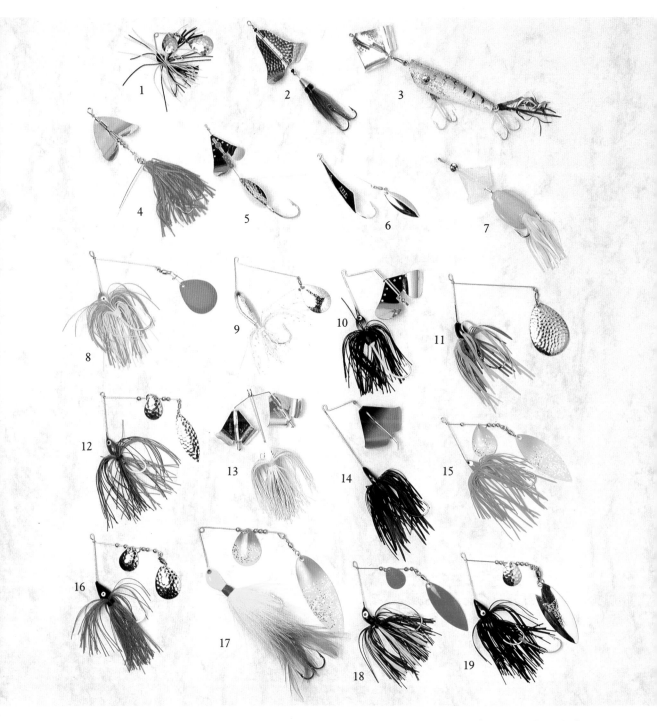

1 Mini-Whacker; 2 Kilty Tri-Lure; 3 Sputterbuzz; 4 Goldwing; 5 Skitter Buzzbait;
6 Arrow Spin; 7 Thundertoad; 8 Little Joe Spinnerbait; 9 Rattlin' Spin R; 10 Clacker;
11 Barrie's Buzzer; 12 Predatory Spinnerbait; 13 Oki Twister; 14 Buzzard; 15 Reed
Runner; 16 Original Roland Martin; 17 Bionic Bucktail; 18 Spoiler; 19 Big Bass.

PLATE E

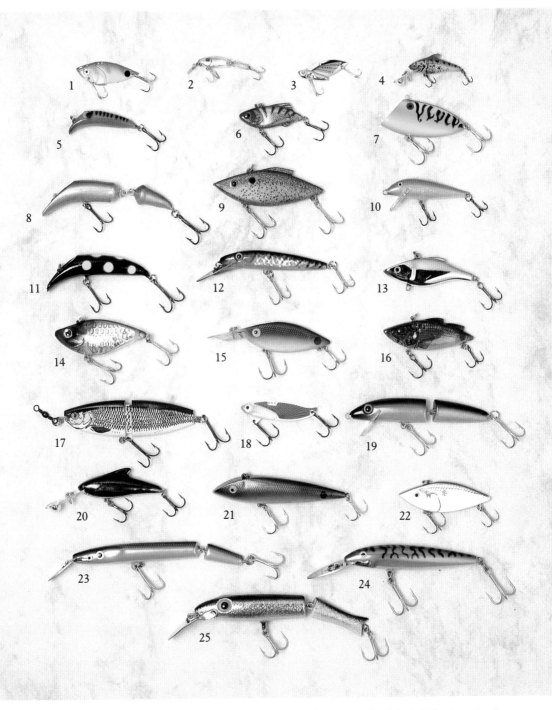

1 Gay Blade; 2 Original Jointed; 3 Cicada; 4 Creek Creature; 5 Little Wiggler; 6 Sugar Shad; 7 Bayou Boogie; 8 Canadian Wiggler (jointed); 9 Rattl' Trap; 10 Countdown; 11 Canadian Wiggler; 12 L-Jack Magnum; 13 Rattl'n Rap; 14 Vibrastar; 15 Longbill Spot; 16 N'Ticer; 17 Jack Rapid; 18 Sonar Flash; 19 L-Jack Jointed Sinking; 20 Wally Demon; 21 Spot Minnow; 22 Spot; 23 Sliver; 24 Magnum Sinker; 25 Jawbreaker.

PLATE F

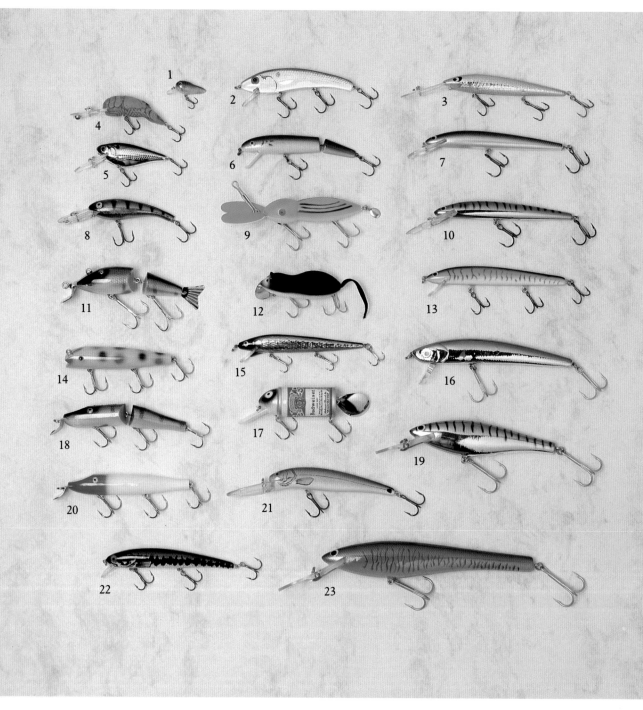

1   Tadfry; 2   Riplin Redfin; 3   Rattlin' Rogue; 4   Crawfish; 5   CC Shad; 6   Jointed Redfin; 7   Bang-O-Lure Diving 5; 8   Wally Diver; 9   Magnum Hellbender; 10   Bang-O-Lure Deep Diving 5; 11   Wiggle Fish; 12   Meadow Mouse; 13   Bang-O-Lure 5; 14   Creek Chub Darter; 15   Hellcat; 16   Top Gun; 17   Big Bud; 18   Creek Chub Pikie (jointed); 19   Bang-O-B 6; 20   Creek Chub Pikie (minnow); 21   Long A Deep Diver; 22   Long A Shallow Diver; 23   Bang-O-B 8.

PLATE G

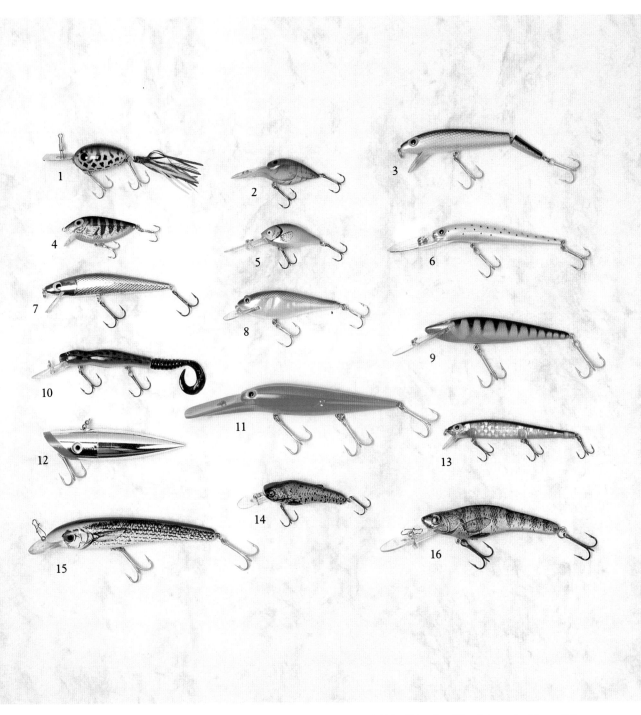

1 Arbogaster; 2 Flat Wart; 3 Jointed Thunderstick; 4 Thin Fin; 5 Hot Lips; 6 Deep JR Thunderstick; 7 Jensen Minnow; 8 Phreds Shadeaux; 9 Snooker Minnow; 10 Super Dawg; 11 Big Mac; 12 J-Plug; 13 Shallow Thunderstick; 14 Bullcat; 15 Javelin; 16 Fingerling.

PLATE H

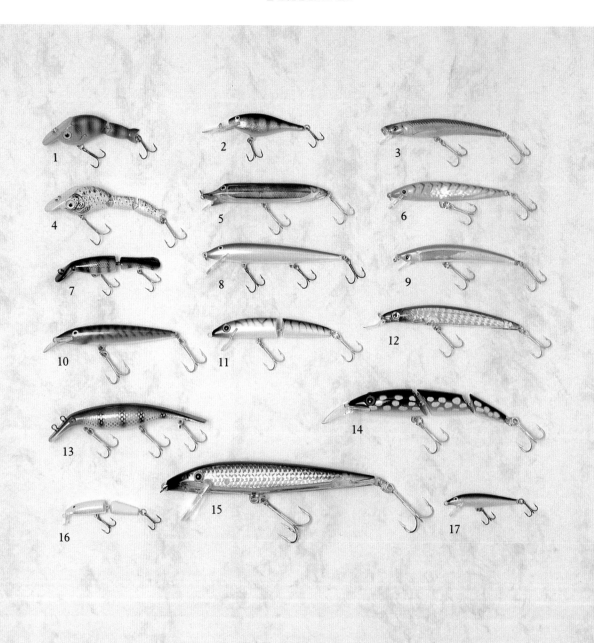

1 Eskimo; 2 Shad Rap; 3 Arc Minnow; 4 Indiana Plug; 5 Special Jack Pike; 6 L-Jack Minnow; 7 Believer; 8 Husky; 9 Crystal Minnow; 10 Magnum (sinking version) ;11 L-Jack Jointed; 12 Dimpstar; 13 Damler (Swim Whiz); 14 Pike Plug – 3 section; 15 Pike Special; 16 Original Jointed Rapala; 17 Original Floating Rapala.

PLATE I

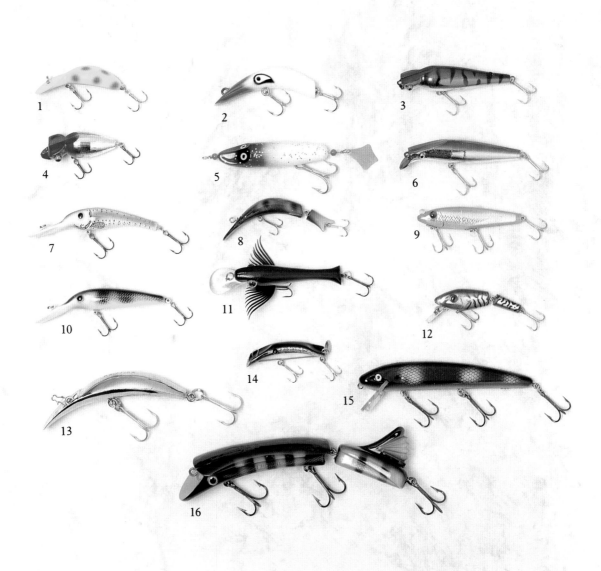

1 Tadpolly; 2 Lazy Ike; 3 Predator; 4 Magna Fat Minnow; 5 Flipper; 6 The Equalizer; 7 Shadling; 8 Limper; 9 Snooker 7; 10 Baitfish; 11 Water Dog; 12 Original Jointed Floating Mirrolure; 13 Kwikfish; 14 Water Lou; 15 Gladiator; 16 Burmek B1.

PLATE J

1 River Runner (Up 'n' Under); 2 Baby Pike Getim (Shakespeare); 3 Conqueror; 4 Oval Sprat; 5 200 Wooden Plug; 6 Spearhead; 7 Devon Minnow; 8 Dapper Dan; 9 Little Jack; 10 Maverick; 11 Invincible; 12 Hi-Lo; 13 Killer Plug; 14 Shimmy.

PLATE K

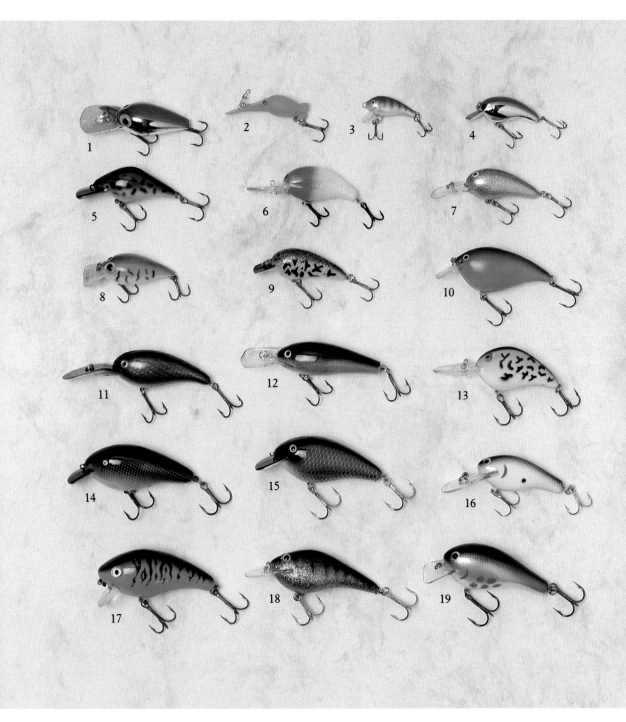

1 Wiggle Wart; 2 Hot Shot; 3 Mini Fat Rap; 4 Minx; 5 Baby Bopper; 6 Harrier; 7 Deep Baby N; 8 Short Wart; 9 Shallow Baby N; 10 Mugger; 11 Hunter; 12 Fat Rap; 13 Fat A; 14 Big Bopper; 15 Big S; 16 B2 Dredge; 17 One Minus; 18 Flash Dancer; 19 Balsa B.

PLATE L

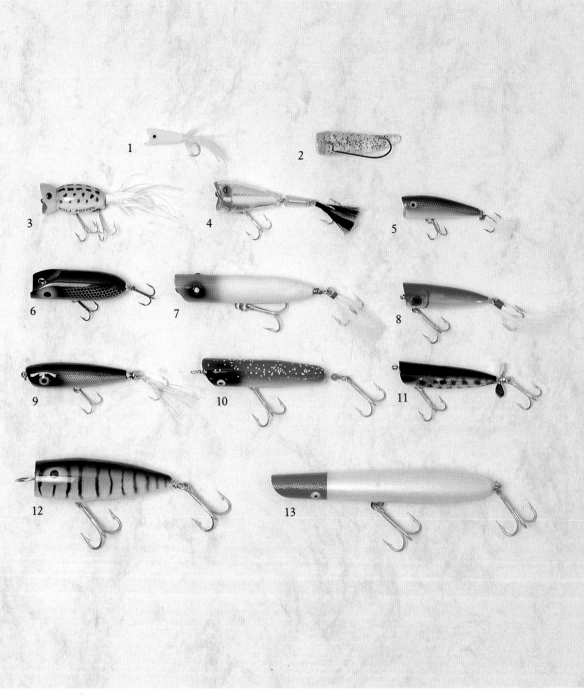

1   Saltwater Bug; 2   Soft Classic Pop-R; 3   Hula Popper; 4   Jointed Surface Popper; 5   Pop-R;
6   Bass Oreno; 7   Striper Striker; 8   Troublemaker; 9   PJ Pop; 10   Silversides;
11   Blabbermouth; 12   Scudder; 13   Pencil Popper.

PLATE M

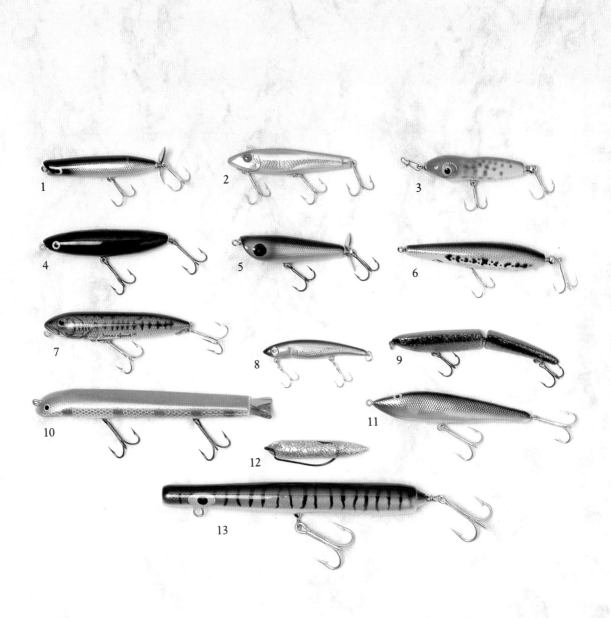

1 Jerk'n Sam; 2 Classic 52MR; 3 Woodwalker; 4 Ugly Albert; 5 Dalton Special;
6 Highroller; 7 Zara Spook; 8 Top 45; 9 Zara Gossa; 10 Thriller; 11 Jumping Snooker;
12 Soft Classic Zara Puppy; 13 Prancer.

PLATE N

1 Crippled Killer; 2   Jitterbug – weedless; 3   Wee Frog; 4   Baby Torpedo; 5   Jitterstick;
6   Natural Frog; 7   Woodchopper; 8   Dying Flutter; 9   Buzz'n Frog; 10   Nip-I- Diddee;
11   Boy Howdy; 12   Bassrat; 13   Crazy Shad; 14   Panatella; 15   Devil's Horse; 16   Scum
Frog; 17   Sinner Spinner; 18   Dasher; 19   Crazy Crawler.

PLATE O

1 Grub; 2 Soft Top Gun; 3 Big Wag; 4 Little Mickey; 5 Flying Lure; 6 CC Spoon;
7 Whistler Jig; 8 Jerk Jigger; 9 Wiggle Jig; 10 Cranked Worm Hook; 11 Bass bug: Frog;
12 Bass bug: Crystal Dragon; 13 Bass bug: Mouse; 14 Bass bug: Beetle; 15 Bass bug: Diving
Shiner; 16 Supershad.

PLATE P

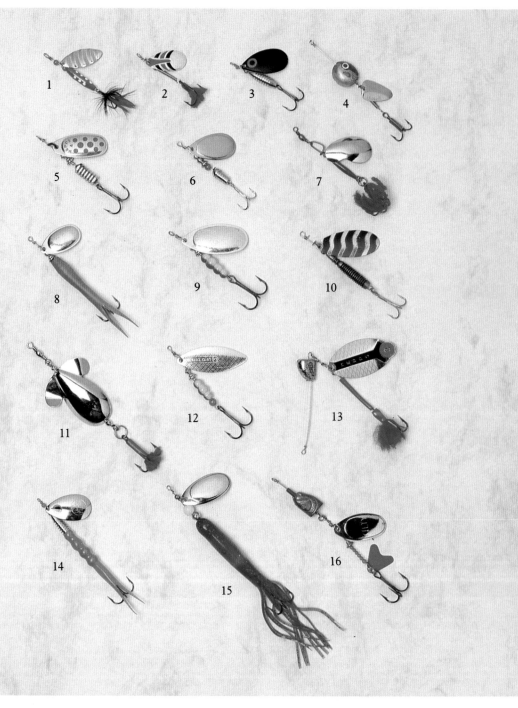

1 Flasher; 2 Ondex; 3 Flipz; 4 Voblex; 5 Comet; 6 Predator Reflex; 7 Kidney Spoon;
8 Aglia Flying C; 9 Aglia; 10 Veltic; 11 Colorado; 12 Aglia Longue; 13 Lusox;
14 Flipz X; 15 Ticklerbait; 16 Steelhead.

Construction   Balsa wood plug with two treble hooks attached via a single section of stainless-steel wire which runs through the body. Distinctive stubby wings near the head.

Colours/finish   Some 58 colours, ranging from silver grey to black, with just about every combination in between. Natural scale finishes are popular.

Sizes   One size; 80mm long, 14g weight.

Use   This unusually shaped plug is a good caster with a tight, refined action. Very responsive, Spearhead dives to 8ft but can be fished at a variety of speeds and depths without sacrificing the action. Try it for trout, salmon and pike.

Special Jack Pike   *PLATE H*

Manufacturer   Yo-Zuri, Japan

Classification   Floating diver

Construction   Long capsule-shaped lure with a sharp snout, large 'teddy bear' eyes, an inset plastic diving vane and two Mustad trebles attached with split rings.

Colours/finish   One colour: a translucent green scale effect on sides, transparent belly.

Sizes   One size: 110mm long, 19g weight.

Use   Special Jack Pike is a straightforward shallow-floating diver with a tight action; with its almost transparent colouring, it is an interesting option for very clear water, when fish may be easily spooked. Finds favour with sea anglers for bassing off the rocks. Widely available.

Others to try   Also available in a sinking version.

Super Dawg   *PLATE G*

Manufacturer   Luhr-Jensen, USA

Classification   Floating diver

Construction   A rather strange-looking reptilian body, with a replaceable soft plastic curled tail. Inset diving vane, two trebles.

Colours/finish   Four colours, all darkish with mottled prints, representing the newt-like salamander.

Sizes   Two sizes: 80mm long, in 11g and 12g versions, the heavier version being the slightly deeper diver.

Use   This medium diver gets down to 7ft and looks rather like a newt or lizard in the water. The soft plastic tail gives a fantastic wriggling motion. Work it with a steady retrieve to make the most of the tail. A really unusual looking plug which should give the fish something to think about, and will certainly ring the changes on a dull day.

Tadfry   *PLATE F*

Manufacturer   Rebel, USA

Classification   Floating diver

Construction   Tadpole-shaped plug with a transparent diving vane. Treble hook attached with a split ring.

Colours/finish   Four colours: Chartreuse Tad, Pink Tad, Shad Tad, Frog Tad.

Sizes   One size: 32mm long, 3g weight.

Use   This ultralite lure is fun for small waters, working from 1–3ft. Fish around

65

holding areas; its ultra buoyant construction means it pops up to the surface when you pause on the retrieve. It's certainly worth trying for trout.

Others to try   Crickhopper (Rebel, USA).

Tadpolly
PLATE I

Manufacturer   Heddon, USA

Classification   Floating diver

Construction   Plastic-moulded, roughly banana-shaped body, with a flattened head acting as the diving vane. Two treble hooks attached with split rings.

Colours/finish   Ten colours, fluorescents, metallic plus a Black Shore Minnow. (The great favourite in the UK, Red Head, has been discontinued.)

Sizes   One size: 73mm long, 14g weight.

Use   This floating diver (8–10ft, casting; 20–22ft, trolling) is an old favourite in the US for salmon and trout. Start the retrieve fast to get the lure down quickly, then fish sink-and-draw style, creating a rising and falling action. One of the original Heddon crankbaits, it's useful where a small, deep diver is needed.

Thin Fin
PLATE G

Manufacturer   Storm, USA

Classification   Floating diver

Construction   Flat cross-sectioned, shad-shaped plug, integral diving vane, large moulded eyes. Two trebles attached with split rings. Rattling version available.

Colours/finish   Over 40 standard colours, but the silvery scale and perch finishes are the outstanding performers in many anglers' estimation.

Sizes   Three floating models and two sinkers, ranging from 64mm long to 90mm long, 14g weight, with diving ranges from 4–8ft.

Use   An excellent small-water lure, Thin Fin dives well and can be relied on to perform just right. The thin fish shape which gives the lure its name gives it a particularly good, tight wiggle. Take care not to overload the trace with heavy hardware when fishing the lighter version – a simple snap suffices. Particularly effective when pike show signs of great hunting activity. Rattlin Thin Fin has a slightly fatter cross-section, to allow for the rattles. A little heavier, it gives a longer casting range and proves especially useful where water is coloured up.

Thunderstick
PLATE G

Manufacturer   Storm, USA

Classification   Floating diver

Construction   Classic, very slim minnow design, big moulded eyes, inset plastic diving vane, two trebles attached with split rings.

Colours/finish   First-class colour range of some 45 finishes – something for every condition – lights, darks, prismatics, chromes, golds and more.

Sizes   A whole family of lures; Standard: 114mm long, 11g weight; JR: 76mm long, 7g weight; Deep JR: 114mm long, 9g weight; Saltwater: 114mm long, 11g weight; Deep: 152mm long, 14g weight; Jointed: 140mm long, 18g weight.

Use   A first-rate minnow family, suitable for pike, bass and pollack. The Jointed Thunderstick is a particular favourite, displaying a startling eel-like action that pike seem to love. Standard shallow Thundersticks dive to around 4ft, the jointed version perhaps slightly less. The Deep Thundersticks will reach 10–14ft comfortably. A strong life-like fishy action makes them very effective in clear water.

Top Gun   *PLATE F*

Manufacturer   Bagley, USA

Classification   Floating diver

Construction   Tough, thick-walled plastic minnow style plug with oversized air chambers – very strong and very buoyant. Large eyes, contoured gills, tough lexan lip and two trebles attached by split rings.

Colours/finish   Twenty colours offering a very wide choice. They are all excellent, reflective and realistic. For pike, the most popular is Tennessee Shad (sometimes listed as Smelt); as for bass and pollack, the blue and silver finishes work well.

Sizes   Two sizes: 114mm long, 10.5g weight; 153mm long, 28g weight.

Use   A very popular lure with a lazy baitfish action plus a constant sonic vibration. The 153mm size is really effective for any situation where a big shallow-running floating diver is wanted. Particularly good for fishing off the rocks for bass and pollack, and for running over kelp beds. One of the few plugs tough enough to be taken on a forthcoming (as we write) Goliath Tigerfish expedition.

Others to try   Also available in a 114mm long deep-diving version, which dives to 16ft.

Up 'n' Under (aka **River Runner**)

PLATE J

Manufacturer   Gordon Griffiths, UK

Classification   Floating diver

Construction   Plastic body, single piece (jointed body soon to be available) inset eyes, 'pike' face. Good solid hook anchorages for the two trebles. Main feature is the Hi-Lo type adjustable lip.

Colours/finish   Six colours: Blue/Green, Red/Black, Yellow/Black, Red Head, Black/Chartreuse, Bright Green.

Sizes   Two sizes: 90mm long, 28g weight, and a chunky 110mm version.

Use   In its flat position, the plug is a deep diver, diving more and more shallowly as the lip is ratcheted up until, with the lip in its vertical position, it will dive just below the surface. A very handy and versatile lure, Up 'n' Under is useful when you're travelling light, as it can do a variety of jobs for you. Casts well; a good plug for the beginner.

Others to try   **Hi-Lo** (Abu, UK).

Wally Demon   *PLATE E*

Manufacturer   Rebel, USA

Classification   Floating diver

Construction   Plastic fish-shaped lure with a distinctive dorsal fin. The large diving lip holds the attachment ring and a ball bearing; two treble hooks attached by split rings.

Colours/finish   Four colours: Silver/Black, Gold/Black, Chartreuse Perch, Stream Demon (bright yellow and green).

Sizes   One size: 90mm long, 14g weight.

Use   This floating diver will dive steeply to 8–10ft, and because the Wally Demon has neutral buoyancy, once there, it will suspend nose down, imitating a feeding fish. Twitch occasionally to attract hungry predators. Also used as a true-running trolling lure.

Others to try   **Deep Diving Rattlin Rogue** (Smithwick, USA).

Wally Diver   PLATE F

Manufacturer   Cordell, USA

Classification   Floating diver

Construction   Fat minnow-shaped plug with fast-tapering tail, moulded eyes, large inset lexan lip and two trebles attached with split rings.

Colours/finish   Range of 20 plus colours from gold/orange to chrome/blue – G-Fleck and G-Finishes included.

Sizes   Two sizes: 57mm long, 7g weight (dives 6–8ft); 108mm long, 11g weight (dives 9–11ft).

Use   This has a slightly larger profile than most minnows, nicely curved towards the tail, which aids good hook setting. Originally designed as a Walleye (Zander) lure (hence the unfortunate name), Wally Diver has become very popular for bass in the US. An excellent long-casting lure, which can also be used for trolling (allow it to touch bottom). Use a hesitant retrieve when casting, making it swim like a small baitfish. Definitely one to try out on zander.

Others to try   **Wally Demon** (Cordell, USA).

Wiggle Fish   PLATE F

Manufacturer   Creek Chub, USA

Classification   Floating diver

Construction   A wooden, jointed floating shallow diver (1–3ft) with a metal diving vane and a ribbed tail fin. Two long shanked trebles.

Colours/finish   Available in Perch only.

Sizes   One size: 115mm long, 26g weight.

Use   This lure was re-issued in 1992 by Creek Chub to commemorate the 60th anniversary of the capture of the world record largemouth bass (22lb 4oz), in Montgomery, Georgia, by George Perry. A perfect replica, packaged in an original style box, the Wiggle Fish is best worked with a steady retrieve; and you can expect it to produce results with pike, perch and chub. The strong wobble is similar to the Creek Chub Pikie. Not only a collector's item, but also a serious lure.

Wiggle Wart   PLATE K

Manufacturer   Storm, USA

Classification   Floating diver

Construction   Flat-bodied shape with a slightly hollow recurve belly, moulded eyes and a large oblong lip. One ball-bearing rattle. Two treble hooks attached with split rings.

Colours/finish   An unbelievable 195 colours are offered, which would take a lifetime to evaluate. However, the natural scale finishes and metallics are a good bet.

Sizes   One size: 76mm long, 10.5g weight.

Use One of the most familiar and most popular of the US crankbaits, this is a medium diver (7–10ft), very stable, whose long lip tends to help avoid snagging. The rattle is enclosed in a transverse chamber, taking advantage of the lure's side-to-side action to produce a good loud noise. In the US, it's used for salmon and steelhead, and also for walleye (zander) trolling. In the UK, it's most commonly used for pike and, in the metallic colours, for perch.

200 Wooden Plug *PLATE J*

Manufacturer Lucky Strike, Canada

Classification Floating diver

Construction Wooden jointed plug with a planed face, screw fitting, three trebles and a metal diving vane.

Colours/finish Ten colours: Yellow Perch is probably the best.

Sizes One size: 108mm long, 20g weight.

Use The number of wooden plugs available gets fewer every year, and perhaps, from an environmental viewpoint, it's a good thing. This classically styled, jointed shallow diver has a smooth, easy action, and will please those who still prefer the buoyancy of wood to plastic. A good general-purpose lure, easy to cast, which will surely take its share of autumn pike.

CHAPTER SIX
VIBRATING LURES

Vibrating lures have a characteristic pointed oval shape; they are lipless, and their attachment point is high on the 'head' of the lure, rather than the more conventional lip-area attachment. These lures vibrate very fast on the retrieve, and tend in the main to be sinkers. They almost all have sound chambers containing ball bearings which rattle as the lure is retrieved. Some rattle so loud that they can actually be heard from the bank!

There is no doubt at all that fish are sensitive to vibration, and at times, they are strongly stimulated by lures which rattle. Sadly, rattles are not an infallible fish attractor, so don't judge a vibrator entirely by the way it rattles in your hand. (When you are assessing the rattle of any lure by shaking it in your hand, don't do the instinctive thing and shake it from head to tail, but try to duplicate its movement in the water, which will almost always be from side to side. Some of the most effective lures have transverse-sounding chambers, rather than just a bunch of ball bearings rattling around.)

Vibrating lures are very versatile; where they fish in the water is down to you. They sink fast, so count them down and start retrieving at the point where you believe the fish to be. If in doubt, search the swim from bottom to top. When you start catching, remember the count and retrieve again from that depth. The usual method is a steady retrieve, but a fast ripping action can also be tried.

All vibrators will cast well, so they are very useful when you're faced with a large expanse of water. One drawback is that they are more likely to get snagged up than buoyant lures with lips, so take care when fishing around obstacles.

———— ♦ ————

Bayou Boogie   PLATE E

Manufacturer   Heddon, USA

Classification   Vibrating lure

Construction   Moulded plastic lipless lure with a raked-back head, a flat face and moulded eyes. Two trebles, a ball-bearing rattle and an attachment eye on top of the lure.

Colours/finish   Twelve mainly natural colours, including two metallics.

Sizes   Just one size in production now: 50mm long, 9g weight.

Use   This classic lure, originally made by Whoppa Stoppa, has been in production for over 45 years. A medium-speed sinker, count it down to the required depth and then retrieve using a decisive lift of the rod tip, which will produce a big vibrating, darting motion. Allow the lure to fall through the water whilst retrieving the slack line. Watch out for takes on the drop. Good for pike, it will also take perch.

Cicada
PLATE E

Manufacturer   Reef Runner, USA

Classification   Vibrating blade/jig

Construction   Moulded metal lure, roughly in the shape of a grasshopper. Two double hooks, with the attachment point on top of the concave wing. Reflecting colour panel on wing.

Colours/finish   A good range of bright metallic colours – gold, pink, purple, etc.

Sizes   Five sizes: 2g, 4g, 7g, 11g, 14g weight.

Use   Another hybrid-type lure, which could be classified as a jig, but is also fished as a vibrator. Fish as a jig in short bounces, and allow to flutter to the bottom, keeping a taut line. Alternatively, cast using a hesitant retrieve with the occasional twitch, or try sink and draw. The larger sizes are easier to use and prove attractive to perch, zander and small pike.

Gay Blade
PLATE E

Manufacturer   Cordell, USA

Classification   Vibrating blade/jig

Construction   Roughly fish-shaped solid metal vibrating lure with moulded gills and a flat planed-off head. Large reflective eye, tail treble hook and double hook located under head, attached direct to the lure. Two attachment points.

Colours/finish   Eight colours: six pale naturals plus a Chartreuse and an Arkansas Shad.

Sizes   Two sizes: 38mm long, 7g weight; 51mm long, 10.5g weight.

Use   Attach by the front point and use a fast retrieve just under the surface to set up a tight vibrating run – attractive to schooling fish. Attach by the rear point and use as a jig for winter pike; works for zander in the US.

Others to try   Sonar Flash (Heddon, USA).

Longbill Spot
PLATE E

Manufacturer   Cordell, USA

Classification   Vibrating lure

Construction   This is the Cordell Spot with an added diving vane. A big rattle, moulded eyes and two trebles attached with split rings.

Colours/finish   A range of 33 good colours, including Neons and G-Flecks.

Sizes   One size: 76mm long, 10.5g weight.

Use   Yet another hybrid lure. This is really a floating diver, but is included in this section since it shares so many characteristics with the Spot. It has a big noisy rattle and fast vibration, with the addition of a lip which will take the lure down to 7ft. This lure allows you to use a variety of techniques, including a conventional retrieve and the usual ripping retrieve used for vibrating lures. Recommended as a salmon lure, it will definitely attract pike, and can be used for light sea spinning.

N-Ticer
PLATE E

Manufacturer   Bill Norman, USA

Classification   Vibrating lure

Construction Fish-shaped vibrating lure with a tapering profile, two dorsal fins, moulded eyes and two treble hooks attached with split rings. Ball-bearing rattles.

Colours/finish Some 43 colours are available; the favourites have reflective cores and fish prints.

Sizes Three sizes: 70mm long, 14g weight; 60mm long, 7g weight; 36mm long, 2.8g weight.

Use Cranked, jigged, or fished sink-and-draw, this is a good, strong vibrating lure, particularly attractive in its smallest size – the Tiny N-Ticer. Best used in deep, clear water.

Rat-L-Trap   *PLATE E*

Manufacturer Bill Lewis, USA

Classification Vibrating lure

Construction Roughly fish-shaped plastic-moulded lure with moulded eyes and a small dorsal fin. Wider at the nose than at the tail, it's filled with ball bearings to create the famous rattle.

Colours/finish Comes in a huge range of colours. Some of the natural Shad colours are real works of art.

Sizes Five sizes: from 3.5g up to 35g weight.

Use Probably the original rattling, vibrating lure, and generally reckoned to be one of the best performers. This lure is so loud that you can hear it rattling underwater as you reel in. Various retrieves can be used for this, as for all vibrating lures; the manufacturers rate the simple 'burn-it', or cast-and-reel fast

retrieve as the most effective. For counting down, the Rat-L-Trap falls at 1½ft per second.

This lure comes in a wide range of versions, from the Tiny Trap at just 3.5g to the Super-Trap at 35g, which means you can get familiar with the action of the lure, and then scale up and down as circumstances dictate, whilst preserving your knowledge of how the lure best works for you.

Others to try   Divin' Rat-L-Trap (Bill Lewis, USA) – Rat-L-Trap becomes crankbait.

Rattl'n Rapala   *PLATE E*

Manufacturer Rapala, Finland

Classification Vibrating lure

Construction This vibrating lure is a solidly built plastic moulding with a built-in rattle. Two treble hooks; metallic finish.

Colours/finish   Six colours: Chrome, Bream, Shad, Chrome Blue, Orange, Fire Tiger.

Sizes Three sizes: 50mm long, 12g weight; 70mm long, 16g weight; 80mm long, 23g weight.

Use Rattl'n Rapala has a very tight shivering action. It can be fished sink-and-draw style, with the rod tip up, or in a fast, ripping series of jerks. It sinks quickly, so care must be taken to avoid snagging the bottom – all vibrators tend to snag up more easily than lipped lures. Best fished from a boat, down into deep water.

Others to try   Spot (Cordell, USA).
Rattl' Trap (Bill Lewis, USA).

Rattling Sonar Flash   *PLATE E*

Manufacturer   Heddon, USA

Classification   Vibrating blade lure

Construction   A roughly fish-shaped coated metal blade with two trebles and three attachment positions on the back of the lure. A large bulbous painted eye chamber encloses the rattle.

Colours/finish   Six colours: chartreuse, pink, gold, silver, green, and blue, all with a highly reflective finish.

Sizes   One size: 48mm long, 7g weight.

Use   A vibrator/jig spoon, this sinking lure has three attachment holes, allowing the angler to use this lure in various ways. Attach by the front hole for shallow running and the best vibration, by the middle hole for jigging and by the rear hole for deeper running and a slower, more wobbling action. It can also be used with an up-and-down jigging motion in deep water, from a boat. Though mainly used for pike in the UK, Dutch friends use them extensively (and with great success) for zander.

Spot (formerly called Rattl' Spot)   *PLATE E*

Manufacturer   Cordell, USA

Classification   Vibrating lure

Construction   Slab-sided, pointed oval-shaped sinking lure. Attachment on top of lure, two treble hooks attached by split ring, multiple rattles.

Colours/finish   Thirty colours (not all sizes available in all colours), mainly naturals plus some metallics, 15 in G-Finish. Favourites include Bronze Bass and Smokey Shad.

Sizes   One of the few lures still available in a wide range of sizes. Five sizes are available, ranging from an ultra-light 50mm long, 7g weight to a chunky 114mm long, 28g weight.

Use   The Spot, with its loud rattle, high speed vibration and long casting capability, is one of the most popular vibrators. Well balanced, the middle-range sizes sink at around 1ft per second, and are recommended for fishing between 1 and 15ft. The Spot can be used for the whole range of predatory fish – from ultra-lights for trout, through to the very largest size for surf casting. Fish it like a jig across the bottom, or use a conventional jerking retrieve.

Others to try   Neon Spots (Cordell, USA) have an internal 'G-Film' which flashes and reflects light – good to try in murky conditions.

Spot Minnow   *PLATE E*

Manufacturer   Cordell, USA

Classification   Vibrating lure

Construction   A longer, slightly wider version of the Cordell Spot. Moulded plastic body, lipless, two trebles attached by split rings, ball-bearing rattles.

Colours/finish   Twelve colours, mainly pale naturals, plus five G-Finishes.

Sizes   Three sizes: 48mm long, 3.5g weight; 83mm long, 7g weight; 108mm long, 21g weight.

Use   The Spot Minnow has a life-like vibrating action, and its long fishy profile rings the changes on the usual vibrating-lure style. Larger than most vibrating lures, it perhaps matches more closely the size and shape of the staple diet of the bigger fish in the swim. A reliable long caster, it is also a good, true-tracking troller.

Sugar Shad PLATE E

Manufacturer   Luhr-Jensen, USA

Classification   Vibrating lure

Construction   Natural fish-shaped, head-weighted lure, complete with anal and dorsal fins. Painted eyes, two VMC treble hooks attached with split rings. Loud rattle.

Colours/finish   Sixteen colours, most of which are foil-based; Copper Crawfish and Silver/Black are particularly appealing.

Sizes   Three sizes are available: 50mm long, 3.5g weight; 63mm long, 7g weight; 80mm long, 14g weight.

Use   Sinks at a rate of 1ft every 2 seconds at a 45-degree angle (due to the weighted head). Has a good wiggling motion in all phases of use, even on the drop, and runs very straight and true. Though it can be used successfully just by simply casting and retrieving, it's more effective if you count down to the required depth and then retrieve a few feet at a time, pausing for a second or two to allow any

following fish to strike. Sugar Shad can also be jigged along the bottom, where it will adopt a head-down, 'feeding' position. In the US, it's used for zander, trout and tarpon amongst others, and it's worth trying for any of our predators.

Vibrastar PLATE E

Manufacturer   Yo-Zuri, Japan

Classification   Vibrating lure

Construction   Transparent plastic lure with lead-weighted head, dimpled sides, large silver eyes, body cavity containing assorted coloured plastic beads and two separate head chambers, each containing a ball bearing. Two Mustad trebles giving a good, solid feel to this lure.

Colours/finish   Two colours: gold and silver.

Sizes   One size: 75mm long, 18g weight.

Use   This very attractive-looking lure has a complicated structure, offering three separate sources of sound and vibration from the three sound chambers. Fish sink-and-draw style – a steady swimming action and even depth will be maintained on the draw phase. The Vibrastar can be fished with a fast ripping motion, but this may be a less effective method for this lure. Try it for pike and zander.

CHAPTER SEVEN

SINKING MINNOWS

Sinking minnows tend to be sinking versions of floating plugs, and chances are it's the floating version you'll try first. The action of a sinking plug in comparison to its floating counterpart will tend to be a little tighter, but the sinking minnow does get down to the desired depth much more quickly and directly. Some specialized sinking lures are particularly valuable in heavy, fast rivers like the Severn and the Wye and on some of the UK's larger salmon rivers.

Generally, when fishing at depths greater than 10–15ft, it may be easier to count down a sinker than to crank down a floater, and because the lure is sinking more or less straight down, you end up fishing for a longer time and distance at the depth you want. (When fishing with any sinking lure, don't close the bail arm until the lure has reached the depth you're aiming for, or you risk the lure penduluming back towards you under the water on too short a line.)

Remember that sinking minnows as well as floaters operate to a maximum depth depending on their design and your tackle set-up. They will, of course, sink to the bottom under their own weight when cast out, and on the retrieve will begin their attracting swimming action as they reach the operating depth.

———— ◆ ————

Canadian Wiggler   *PLATE E*

Manufacturer   Lindquist Bait Co, Canada

Classification   Sinking diver

Construction   Curved-bodied plug made from brass tubing, with attachment eye and hook rings brazed in place to give a very solid sinking lure. VMC trebles.

Colours/finish   Some 43 colours obtainable, ranging from Chrome, Red Head and Yellow Belly through to the more unusual fluorescents like Shocking Pink.

Sizes   Eight sizes available: 127mm long, 39g weight, MJ (jointed); 102mm long, 28g weight, M (jointed); 102mm long, 21g weight, CWJ (jointed); 83mm long, 14g weight, CW; 60mm long, 7g weight, S; 38mm long, 4g weight, J; 60mm long, 2g weight, SF (floater); 83mm long, 14g weight, CWR (rattling sinker).

Use   Originally brought into the UK as a salmon lure, since it is used extensively for salmon in the rivers and lakes of Canada, the Wiggler was quickly discovered by the pike fraternity as an excellent deep-water, long-casting sinking plug. Very useful in situations where you are fishing deep narrow waters, such as some of the big drains, as you eliminate the wasted fishing territory created by cranking down a floating diver. With its side-to-side wobble, typical of the banana-shaped lure, it appeals to any number of fish; we have recently heard of the capture of a 6lb chub on a Wiggler. Apart from chrome, no really good metallic finishes are presently offered, but those who like flashy lures have been known to strip down one of their least favoured

Wigglers with strong paint stripper to get down to the original metal, which is then cleaned up to achieve a dazzling finish.

Countdown   *PLATE E*

Manufacturer   Rapala, Finland

Classification   Sinking diver

Construction   Weighted balsa minnow, slow sinker, sturdy hook anchorage points for two trebles.

Colours/finish   Nine colours; orange is particularly attractive.

Sizes   Eight sizes; minnow: 30mm long, 3g weight; 50mm long, 5g weight; 70mm long, 8g weight; 90mm long, 11g weight; 110mm long, 16g weight; jointed: 70mm long, 7g weight; 90mm long, 11g weight; 110mm long, 15g weight.

Use   The lure's name is based on the idea that sinking lures can be counted down to a certain depth by counting to, say 6, before commencing the retrieve. By waiting for the same count each cast, you ensure you fish the same depth, cast after cast. Another good lure for all predators, but best in still water for perch, chub and pike in the larger sizes. Much used also for salmon; widely available.

Creek Creature   *PLATE E*

Manufacturer   Rebel, USA

Classification   Sinking diver

Construction   Plastic fish-shaped plug (like a tiny Wally Diver) with a large diving lip weighted with a ball bearing. Two trebles attached with split rings.

Colours/finish   Four colours: Creek Devil, Stream Demon, Phantom Pink, Mad Tom Blue.

Sizes   One size: 38mm long, 3.5g weight.

Use   This ultralite sinking lure has a weighted diving lip which means it comes to rest nose down, imitating a feeding fish; twitch it gently along the bottom. On light tackle, this is a popular lure for small water trout and is also suitable for perch and chub.

Others to try   Cat'r Crawler (Rebel, USA).

Deep Tracdown Wee Crawfish   *PLATE F*

Manufacturer   Rebel, USA

Classification   Sinking diver

Construction   Natural crayfish-shaped plug, with pincers extended. Large diving vane with a captive steel ball positioned at the rear of the lure to place crayfish in a natural position when at rest. Two treble hooks attached with split rings.

Colours/finish   Eight colours, all fairly natural (except a screaming fluorescent red, which can work well in coloured water).

Sizes   One size: 63mm long, 14g weight.

Use   This slow-sinking crawfish plug can be fished on the bottom at depths of up to 15ft. A normal cast and a medium-speed, steady retrieve, means that the lure will run at around 10ft. Useful for fishing where crayfish are present, but will be readily taken by fish which have never seen a crayfish in their lives. Can also be used as a trolling lure. A very useful sea lure which does a good imitation of a prawn.

Others to try There is a whole family of floating diver Wee-Crawfish lures, from the ultralite Teeny Wee Crawfish to the Deep Wee Crawfish: worth trying if your local fish seem to like the crayfish shape.

Jack Rapid
PLATE E

Manufacturer VLC, Denmark (distributed by Ryobi)

Classification Sinking diver

Construction Solid plastic, hinged in the middle. Extremely thin profile, tiny balancing fins at the tail and two trebles attached with copper split rings, very firmly anchored. Strongly made and highly resistant to attack.

Colours/finish Ten colours: red, green, blue, yellow, and black on either white or grey, complete with a fish print.

Sizes Two sizes: 82mm long, 8g weight; 104mm long, 28g weight.

Use An unusual lure, relatively new to the UK market, and offering a fantastically realistic fish action. Casts extremely well; a steady retrieve produces the best action. Should be widely available.

Jawbreaker
PLATE E

Manufacturer Rebel, USA

Classification Sinking diver

Construction Moulded foam body, with a stainless-steel, double-anchored diving vane, two 3X cadmium-plated treble hooks attached with split rings, linked by a stainless-steel harness which is moulded inside the body of the

lure, and which also links to the nose ring. The belly hook is anchored with a 250lb rated swivel, designed to prevent the fish using the lure's body as leverage to throw the hooks. A very tough plug.

Colours/finish Six colours, based on silver or chartreuse. (Large size available in silver-based colours only.)

Sizes Two sizes, both coming jointed or straight: 140mm, 28g and 177mm, 63g.

Use A big fish lure designed for trolling, which runs true even at speed. Primarily designed for sea fish, this could be a good choice for pike, loch salmon and ferox.

L-Jack Jointed Sinking
PLATE E

Manufacturer Yo-Zuri, Japan

Classification Sinking diver

Construction Very solid construction: stainless steel wired through, large 'teddy bear' eyes, transparent plastic inset diving vane and two Mustad trebles attached with split rings.

Colours/finish Three colours: gold, silver and mackerel.

Sizes Three sizes: 90mm long, 14g weight; 110mm long, 20g weight; 130mm long, 32g weight.

Use Originally designed for sea use, this robust lure is an equally good addition to the pike armoury. Count it down to the taking depth and retrieve at slow-to-medium speed, occasionally allowing the lure to drop back. An undramatic but effective action; widely available.

L-Jack Magnum

PLATE E

Manufacturer Yo-Zuri, Japan

Classification Sinking diver

Construction Very tough transparent plastic lure, with stainless steel wired through the body. Large 'teddy bear' eyes, inset pointed heavy metal diving vane and two Mustad trebles attached with split rings. A prismatic strip embedded along its length creates a 'flash' effect as the lure moves.

Colours/finish Four colours, all variations on gold and blue.

Sizes Five sizes: 70mm long, 7.5g weight; 90mm long, 11g weight; 110mm long, 18g weight; 130mm long, 27g weight; 170mm long, 55g weight.

Use This lure was designed with big game sea fishing in mind (tuna and barracuda amongst others), and it's certainly built to withstand the kind of treatment such fish can give. The metal lip will stand up well to fishing over rock, where plastic can sometimes break. The smaller sizes could be very useful for fishing fast, deep water, where it's hard to get a lure down to the taking depths – piking in parts of the Severn for instance.

Magnum Sinker

PLATE E

Manufacturer Rapala, Finland

Classification Sinking diver

Construction A very robust sinking version of the Magnum. Big metal lip on a solid Odum wood body, two trebles.

Colours/finish Five colours; Green Mackerel is particularly good looking.

Sizes Available in four sizes: 90mm long, 17g weight; 110mm long, 24g weight; 140mm long, 36g weight; 180mm long, 58g weight.

Use Ideal for sea trolling, and also used for freshwater trolling in the UK. Very stable and reliable action, suitable for big pike, salmon as well as sea predators. Unlike many big-game lures, even the larger Magnums are not too big for heavy pike fishing.

Original Jointed

PLATE E

Manufacturer Mirrolure, USA

Classification Sinking diver

Construction Jointed minnow-shaped lure with realistic eyes, narrow oblong metal diving vane, two trebles.

Colours/finish Some 35 colours, all with a reflective finish; wide choice of both bright and natural colours.

Sizes Available in four sizes: 41mm long, 2g weight; 51mm long, 4g weight; 63mm long, 7g weight; 76mm long, 11g weight.

Use This lure is particularly good in its two smallest versions. It has a very lifelike wiggling action, and is a great little hunter, working at between 2 and 5ft. Try it for chub and perch, but don't forget that you need a trace, no matter how light, as pike will happily take this little chap.

Sliver

PLATE E

Manufacturer Rapala, Finland

Classification Sinking diver

Construction Another tough customer, the Sliver is made from hard Odum wood and, as its name suggests, has a very slim profile. Metal lip, marine quality hooks.

Colours/finish Seven colours: Silver, Blue, Orange, Blue Mackerel, Chartreuse, Red-head, Gold/Green.

Sizes Two sizes: 130mm long, 16g weight (sinks 10–12ft); 200mm long, 42g weight (sinks 12–14ft).

Use An excellent finish and tight fish-like action make this a top class lure, at its best trolled. Used for big game fish in warm seas, it will take pike, salmon and most predators. A must for the serious troller; widely available.

Water-Lou   *PLATE I*

Manufacturer Queen City Tackle Co, USA

Classification Sinking diver

Construction Banana-shaped, solid plastic

plug with a flattened head and tail and moulded eyes. The hooks are attached to a stainless-steel harness which runs underneath the lure from head to tail. Small flicker spinner at tail.

Colours/finish Range of 27 colours, many with an encapsulated glitter effect. A good selection, perhaps a little short on dull naturals, but compensating with some good flashy offerings – Pike, Perch and Carp are particularly attractive. (Not all colours are available in the ultralite version.)

Sizes Four sizes, ranging from the 25mm long, less than 1g weight Ultralite version to the 82mm long, 17.5g weight senior version.

Use A sinking lure with a darting action, suitable for casting or trolling (with weight added up the line). The unusual hooking system makes the lure easy to tune, and the little tail spinner gives the Water-Lou that extra bit of flash. A slow retrieve gives the best action. First produced in 1947, it's popular in the US for salmon and pike.

CHAPTER EIGHT
SPINNERS

Spinners cover yet another very large category of lures, which, superficially at least, can look very similar. (Don't be misled by the description 'bar spoon' – this is in fact a spinner, as is a 'fly spoon'.) The basic structure of a spinner is a revolving blade attached to a central axis coupled with some kind of weight and often with a fish-attracting addition such as a hackle or a rubber skirt.

Spinners have blades of differing shapes which offer differing actions. Broadly speaking, the narrower the blade, the faster and closer to the lure body it revolves and the deeper the lure can work. The strongest vibrations come from the widest blade shapes. these have more water resistance and so revolve more slowly and at a wider angle from the axis. They can be fished higher up in the water, making them suitable for shallow and slow-flowing swims.

The commonest shapes are as follows: the long, pointed Willow blade, shaped like a willow leaf, the almost round Colorado blade, the teardrop-shaped Indiana Blade, the French blade, which has a more regular oval shape, and the Sonic blade, leaf-shaped and designed to fit directly on to the central axis rather than being attached with a clevis.

Generally, the spinner has its weight behind the blade, for example the Mepps Aglia, but there are some well known versions with the weight in front of the blade (the most familiar of these is probably the Voblex).

Blades are available in a huge variety of colours and finishes, from the standard gold, silver, copper and brass through to painted, fluorescent, pearl, etched and many other versions. There are many theories about colour, and few facts! However, it seems likely that in clear water, colour and flash play their part, and gold and silver are consistent producers for most people. Experimenting is part of the fun, so it's worth trying different combinations, and in particular, trying to match the colour of the lure to the natural food that's around.

As far as size is concerned, try to match the lure to the size of the food on which your quarry is likely to be feeding. It therefore follows that small spinners tend to be used for smaller fish, and large ones for the likes of pike. The fish don't necessarily know these rules, however: big fish are still caught on small lures and small ones on big lures.

One important thing to remember is that spinners *spin*, and unless you use a good, free-running swivel at the end of your trace, you will end up with a badly kinked line.

Spinners are relatively easy to use; a steady retrieve is needed to keep the blade turning. You will know when you've got it right, because you will feel the vibration of the blade through your rod. If you feel that vibration stop, you're going too slowly, you're weeded up or you've got a fish!

———— ◆ ————

Aglia
PLATE P

Manufacturer Mepps, France

Classification Spinner

Construction Bar spoon with a classic French pattern blade. Wide angle (60 deg) rotation around the axis. Treble hook.

Colours/finish Comes in many variants. Aglia is available in a number of blade colours: Copper, Silver, Gold and Black with red, blue or black dots, with or without red wool tassels on the hook. Plain fluorescent blades are also offered, as is a model with a trailing, soft rubber minnow.

Sizes Seven sizes, from 1.5g to 13g.

Use A short-range spinner, which tends to lift in the water because of its wide action blade, making it suitable for use in shallow water. Use a steady retrieve. Probably the UK's top selling and most popular spinner, it is widely available, at least in the basic version, though the variants may take more hunting down.

Others to try **Aglia Decoree, Fluo, Mouche, TW**, (Mepps, France). **Dorado, Jet, Pearl** (Shakespeare, UK). **Attacker, Fizzi Kill, Jupiter, Victor** (Daiwa, UK).

Aglia Flying C   *PLATE P*

Manufacturer Mepps, France

Classification Spinner

Construction Front-weighted body and French-style Aglia blade attached with clevis. Tubular rubber body, treble hook.

Colours/finish Blade colours: Black, Silver, Copper and Gold. Body colours: Red or Natural (light, creamy brown).

Sizes Three sizes: 10g, 15g and 25g.

Use Many people (though not Mepps) claim to have originated the Flying C (or Flying Condom, as this style of spinner was originally named) and versions abound. This is a very long-casting, fast-sinking lure with a very free, revolving wide-angled blade (60 deg). The cut ends of the rubber sleeve flutter like a tail. Fish in deep, fast water, or in shallower water keeping the rod tip up and a fast-ish rate of retrieve. It's absolutely devastating for salmon and sea trout, and also proves very good for pike. In the US, they stuff the rubber body with cotton wool soaked in attractants such as pilchard oil, to create a trail of exciting smell in the water. A very long casting lure, it's extremely useful in high winds. This style of lure should feature in just about everyone's lure box.

Others to try Original Flying C (Kilty, Ireland).

Aglia Longue   *PLATE P*

Manufacturer Mepps, France

Classification Spinner

Construction Long, narrow, willow-leaf blade; red and yellow metal triple-bead body; treble hook.

Colours/finish Blade available in Gold, Silver or Copper.

Sizes Eight sizes: 0, 1.5g; 00, 2.5g; 1, 4.5g; 1+, 5g; 2, 6g; 3, 11g; 4, 17.5g; 5, 29g.

Use This classic spinner has been around for as long as most anglers have! The willow-leaf blade rotates around its axis at an angle of around 30 deg, giving it the silhouette of a small fish when it's in motion. A heavy vibration allows you to keep contact with the lure – when it stops, it may be due to weed, but it may also be a fish, so stay alert. A medium-pace, steady retrieve should be used; choose the Longue for fast-flowing or deep water, where it will get down to the bottom easily and will not plane up in the water.

Others to try   The Aglia Longue also comes dressed with a hackle – the **Aglia Longue Mouche** – and with a tiny rubber fish – the **Mini Rainbo Saumon** – as well as two blade variants: the **Rainbow** and the **Redbo**.

Bang Tail   *PLATE C*

Manufacturer   Luhr-Jensen, USA

Classification   Spinner

Construction   Willow blade attached by a large clevis; slim, solid, parallel-sided body, built-in swivel, hackle and separate straight point VMC treble hook.

Colours/finish   Available in 19 colours, including a silver-plated version, the Silver Bullet. All blades have a reflective scalite finish.

Sizes   Seven sizes, ranging from the 1.75g version to the 80mm long, 14g version.

Use   A very free-running spinner designed for quick blade pick-up and suitable for all predatory species. Produces a good vibrating throb that keeps you in touch with the lure. This quality lure is a little lighter for its size than the similar Rooster Tail, and will be effective at slightly shallower depths.

Colorado Spoon   *PLATE P*

Manufacturer   Allcocks, UK

Classification   Spinner

Construction   Spoon blade with two stubby, oppositely-angled fins, through which runs a weighted axial bar. Quality swivel, treble hook dressed with red wool.

Colours/finish   Nickel, with the concave side of the spoon and the axial bar painted red.

Sizes   Six sizes: 25mm, 32mm, 38mm, 44mm, 51mm, 64mm.

Use   A very traditional spinner which has been around for years, and may be overlooked in the midst of more fashionable offerings. It has a very strong spinning action, and the alternate flashes of red and silver are thought to be attractive to pike. With care, it can be fished high up in the water, or allowed to sink and fished with a medium retrieve at depth.

Comet Decoree   *PLATE P*

Manufacturer   Mepps, France

Classification   Spinner

Construction   Bar spoon, with stretched French-pattern blade with 45 deg rotation from axis. Treble hook.

Colours/finish   Available in Gold, Silver or Copper with red or blue spots. Plain blades also available.

Sizes   Seven sizes, from 1.5g to 13g.

Use   A short-range, medium-depth, general-purpose spinner for all predatory species. Runs deeper than the Aglia, but not as deep as the Aglia Longue.

Others to try   **Black Fury, Comet Rainbow** (Mepps; France).

Droppen *PLATE C*

Manufacturer   Abu Garcia, UK

Classification   Spinner

Construction   Indiana blade with crimped edge, a bomb-shaped body and a fly-dressed treble hook.

Colours/finish Seven colours, including black blades with yellow, blue or green markings.

Sizes   Available in 4g, 6g, 8g, 12g and 18g.

Use   Despite the weight range, the Droppen is a small spinner, the extra weight being balanced at the back of the central body. This, and the fact that Droppen is a heavy lure for its size, makes it an excellent long-casting spinner on light tackle. Because of its size, Droppen is most popular for perch, trout and chub, although many a young pike angler started his lure-fishing career with a Droppen. Particularly good for fast-flowing water and deep lakes.

Flasher *PLATE P*

Manufacturer   Intrepid, UK

Classification   Spinner

Construction   Fluted blade revolving around a painted bar, with an attractive fly-hackle dressing a Mustad treble hook.

Colours/finish   Only available in silver with Red/Black hackle.

Sizes   Two sizes available: 7g, 12g weight.

Use   A useful, low-cost fly spinner, decently made, suitable for small water work. Widely available.

Flipz *PLATES P AND B*

Manufacturer   Landa Sport, UK

Classification   Spinner

Construction   Colorado blade with big contrasting eye, neatly turned brass body, good treble.

Colours/finish   Six colours are offered: the usual gold/silver combinations plus fluorescent red and yellow blades, and an unusual black blade. All are of very high quality.

Sizes   Five sizes: from 2g up to 7g.

Use   These are lightweight spinners suitable for perch, sea trout and small pike. Essentially short-range lures, these will score well on small waters. You'll probably be able to find these in your local shops.

Others to try   **Predatory Reflex** (Middy, UK).

Flipz X *PLATE P*

Manufacturer   Landa Sport, UK

Classification   Spinner

Construction   Flying C-type lure, brass body with four additional beads (two on smaller size), Colorado blade spinner with large eye, treble hook.

Colours/finish   Four body colours: Red, Yellow, Black and Clear. Four blade colours: Copper, Gold, Fluorescent Orange and Fluorescent Yellow.

Sizes   Available in two sizes: 9g and 13g.

Use An excellent variation on the Flying Condom theme (the bulging bead body creates added vibration). Very light blade and clevis result in good pick up through the water. Good, long rubber tail. Popular amongst salmon anglers, and especially useful in fine water conditions.

Flyer *PLATE C*

Manufacturer Abu Garcia, UK

Classification Spinner

Construction The Flyer has a big body for its overall size. Unusual tapered blade, attached by the 'thick' end. Treble hook dressed with jungle cock feathers.

Colours/finish Five colour blades available, including three fluorescent with black stripes, body black with gold spots.

Sizes Available in two sizes only: 7g and 12g.

Use The Flyer is a good perch, chub and salmon lure and a very long-casting lure for its size.

Flyer Jig *PLATE C*

Manufacturer Abu Garcia, UK

Classification Spinner

Construction Barrel-shaped body. Front-mounted 'wavy' propeller, medium-sized single hook with soft plastic grub trailing.

Colours/finish Two colours are offered: Silver/Black and Fluorescent Orange.

Sizes Three sizes: 7g, 10g and 15g.

Use This is a relatively new type of lure to the UK, but perch, chub and trout are likely to take a close interest in the very life-like worm trailing behind the spinner. This is really a hybrid buzzbait/spinner, the blade being somewhat smaller and differently shaped from the usual buzzbait winged prop, and the lure working under, as well as on, the surface. Would also be a useful inshore lure for mackerel and bass.

Hot'N'Tot Pygmy *PLATE C*

Manufacturer Storm, USA

Classification Weight-forward spinner

Construction Fish-shaped lead body with 'Prismflash' eyes, based on the Hot'N'Tot plug design. Heavy gauge stainless-steel wire, French blade, two multi-faceted plastic beads, single hook.

Colours/finish Eighteen colours, all very bright, with silver blade and contrasting colour beads.

Sizes Three sizes: 10.5g weight, 17.5g weight and 24.5g weight (length 185mm overall).

Use This is a really long caster; the fish body wiggles from side to side in the water, and the blade creates a butterfly flutter behind it. Cast out and allow to sink to the desired depth, then fish with a sink-and-draw type retrieve – takes will often occur on the sink phase of the retrieve. Add extra attraction with a skirt or plastic worm. The larger size will get you down quickly to where the fish may be lying, in very deep water.

Kidney Spoon
PLATE P

Manufacturer   Allcocks, UK

Classification   Spinner (confusingly called a bar spoon).

Construction   Classic, kidney-shaped blade, the convex face silver and the concave face red, revolving around a central axis, with a weighted, red painted bar adding weight. Treble hook traditionally dressed with a red wool hackle.

Colours/finish   Silver/red only.

Sizes   Six sizes: 25mm, 32mm, 38mm, 44mm, 51mm and 64mm long.

Use   An old-fashioned style spinner dating back many years, but still deadly for pike, and not to be ignored amidst the plethora of new ideas. A medium retrieve is needed for this one; it will collapse if reeled in too slowly.

Lotto
PLATE C

Manufacturer   Nils Master, Finland

Classification   Spinner

Construction   Fish-shaped oval body with moulded gills and eyes. Indiana blade with a shaped end, attached by a clevis. Treble hook.

Colours/finish   Eleven colours, the favourites being the natural scale versions. Blades are copper, gold or silver and matched with appropriate body colour.

Sizes   Three sizes: 35mm long, 9g weight; 45mm long, 12g weight; 60mm long, 15g weight.

Use   This is an excellent little spinner which is both easy to fish and productive, the kind of lure which boosts confidence on a bad day. The body travels through the water flat, and the lure can be fished at a variety of speeds without losing performance. Accurate in casting, the action is very busy and attracts all species, particularly perch, trout and chub.

Lusox
PLATE P

Manufacturer   Mepps, France

Classification   Weight-forward spinner

Construction   Straight bar body. Oval blade with angled sides and flattened end creating a three-faced effect, removable lead fish head, treble hook dressed with red wool.

Colours/finish   Blade colours are Gold, Silver and Black.

Sizes   Four sizes: 7g, 12g, 16g, 21g.

Use   The Lusox was specifically designed as a pike lure, but it's also proved very successful for perch over recent seasons. The lead head keeps the lure well down, and allows the blade to begin a fluttering rotation as soon as it hits the water. At a constant rate of retrieve, the blade revolves at a 25 deg angle around the axis. This, combined with the fish head, gives the lure a fishy appearance. Can be fished very shallow if the lead head section is removed.

Others to try   GV (Mepps, France). This has a variable geometry blade, which creates a more erratic action.

Ondex
PLATE P

Manufacturer   Rublex, France

Classification   Spinner

Construction Indiana-bladed, lightweight bar spoon. Treble hook, available with or without red wool dressing.

Colours/finish Available in silver, gold or copper blades, plain, or with a red/black stripe finish.

Sizes Six weights, from 1.5g to 9g.

Use This large, lightweight spinner flutters beautifully on a slow retrieve. Its short casting range is best for shallowish water.

Predatory Reflex Spinner   *PLATE P*

Manufacturer Middy, UK

Classification Spinner

Construction A French blade revolving around a central wire axis. Plastic spacer beads and brass body. The treble hooks appear to vary, some being silver coloured, some bronze.

Colours/finish Blades in Silver, Gold and Copper.

Sizes Available in 3g, 6g and 9g weight.

Use A low-cost, short-range, stillwater spinner which is easy to fish in the upper part of the water. Widely available.

Reflex   *PLATE C*

Manufacturer Abu Garcia, UK

Classification Spinner

Construction A rounded multi-ridged willow blade with a barrel-shaped body and a fly-hackle dressed treble hook.

Colours/finish Nine colours available. The black blade with gold bars is very popular, as is the fluorescent red version with black bars. Bodies are painted either red with white spots, white with black spots or black with red spots.

Sizes Available in 7g, 12g and 18g.

Use Another perch and chub spinner which, because of its small hooks, is not recommended for waters likely to contain pike of any size. An old and tried model, it is even better than Droppen for fast water because of its shape. Very long casting.

Rooster Tail   *PLATE C*

Manufacturer Worden/Yakima Bait Co, USA

Classification Spinner

Construction Narrow, willow-leaf type blade attached with a large clevis. Parallel-sided heavy body. Treble hook or single hook versions, both dressed with a good hackle. (The Ultralite version has a tiny propeller instead of a blade.)

Colours/finish A vast range of 73 colours, which caters for every fishing situation.

Sizes Ten sizes, ranging from the Ultralite, 20mm long, less than 1g in weight to the 70mm long, 28g version.

Use The Rooster Tail offers such a wide range of colours and sizes that it should be possible to match almost any natural food. Heavy and therefore fast sinking, is suited mainly to deep or fast-flowing water, although it also works well jigged in sink-and-draw style. The blade produces a good, strong vibration. Try the small sizes for perch and small trout, the large sizes for salmon, pike and large trout.

Shyster
PLATE C

Manufacturer   Luhr-Jensen, USA

Classification   Spinner

Construction   Fluted blade, barrel body, offset eye and hackle-dressed treble.

Colours/finish   Ten colour schemes, generally bright bodies and fly hackles.

Sizes   Five sizes: 22mm long, 2g weight; 27mm long, 4g weight; 33mm long, 7g weight; 36mm long, 9g weight; 42mm long, 14g weight.

Use   This style of blade falls in between the deep-working, narrow blades and the shallow-working, broad blades, so use this spinner when you are looking for a medium-depth lure. The fluted ridges on the blade are designed to reflect light as well as to create vibration, so this is a lure to use in clear water where this feature has maximum effect. Match the colour of the lure to the natural food you suspect your prey may be hunting.

Snagless Sally
PLATE C

Manufacturer   Hildebrandt, USA

Classification   Spinner

Construction   22k gold-plated Idaho blade (nickel option available) rigged to a 2/0 single Mustad hook trailed by a high quality vinyl or living rubber skirt; features a two-pronged weed guard.

Colours/finish   Choice of fluorescent skirt colours – the red is particularly good, as is the chartreuse. Blades are either 22k gold- or nickel-plated, easy to keep highly polished for maximum flash.

Sizes   Available in four sizes: 4.5g, 7g, 10.5g, 14g.

Use   Sinks, but on retrieve tends to work towards the surface. Start reeling in the moment the lure hits the water where weed is a problem. Suitable for shallow water, particularly over summer weed beds. Good for both freshwater and sea species; try it over the kelp. Not a great caster, but at its best over medium range.

Steelhead
PLATE P

Manufacturer   Kilty, Ireland

Classification   Weight-forward spinner

Construction   A heavy lead head mounted forward on a central stainless-steel wire axis. A good sized French blade, attached by a clevis, rotates around the shaft. Treble hook and red plastic tail fin.

Colours/finish   Two colours: Gold and Silver.

Sizes   Four sizes available: 8g, 14g, 18g and 25g.

Use   A good, weight-forward spinner which, due to its weight, will fish low in the water, the blade giving a good flutter. A long-casting lure, needing a fairly brisk rate of retrieve. Has performed well for cold water pike; try casting it to the deep holes where perch hang out.

Swiss Lunker Minnow
PLATE C

Manufacturer   Renosky, USA

Classification   Spinner

Spinners

Construction   Pointed sonic blade with prismatic decal, gold and red spacer beads, fish print rubber minnow and treble hook under belly.

Colours/finish   Five colours: Perch, Rainbow Trout, Brown Trout, Largemouth Bass, Smallmouth Bass. Blades come with red or silver prism tape.

Sizes   Three sizes: 65mm long, 5g weight; 90mm long, 10g weight; 135mm long, 28g weight.

Use   The very free-spinning sonar blade allows this lure to be fished relatively slowly. The vibration of the blade is said by the manufacturers to activate an oscillating tail motion which imparts a lifelike movement to the minnow. The small sizes will be taken by trout and perch, the large sizes are very effective for pike. Use a steady retrieve, as the lure has little action on the drop, and speed up occasionally to encourage a following fish to attack the lure.

Switcheroo   *PLATE C*

Manufacturer   Hildebrandt, USA

Classification   Spinner

Construction   Colorado blade, barrel-shaped body, snap loop attachment for dressed treble hook.

Colours/finish   Blades available in 24k gold- or nickel-plated finish. Choice of fly colours: Black/Yellow, Red/White, Yellow, Guinea/Yellow.

Sizes   Five sizes: 2g, 3g, 4g, 6g, 7g.

Use   A top quality spinner. The use of a nickel or 24k gold finish means that the blade

can be kept bright and reflective. The snap loop enables hooks to be changed very simply and quickly in response to the needs of the moment. Can be fished slow and high in the water, suitable for shallower water. Attractive to all species, it has been particularly successful in the UK for sea trout.

Ticklerbait   *PLATE P*

Manufacturer   Gordon Griffiths, UK

Classification   Spinner

Construction   French blade revolving around a lead-weighted, soft plastic squirt body, with streamer tails round a treble hook.

Colours/finish   Blades come in Silver, Gold and Copper, squirt bodies in ten colours, Hot Red and Yellow being the most popular.

Sizes   Three sizes: 12g, 21g and 28g weight.

Use   A well liked game lure which also finds some supporters amongst the pike fraternity. The heavy body gives it good casting capabilities; it's particularly suitable for medium-deep, fast-flowing water. Good, free-spinning blade producing an attractive flutter.

Others to try   **Bucktail Tickler** (Gordon Griffiths, UK). Bucktail instead of squirt. **Tickler Buzzbait** (Gordon Griffiths, UK). Similar to Tickler but spinnerbait style.

Tiger Tail   *PLATE C*

Manufacturer   Luhr-Jensen, USA

Classification   Spinner

Construction   The deep, sonar blade revolves around a central shaft; offset eye. Bullet-

88

shaped body, treble hook dressed with hackle.

Colours/finish   A range of 15 colours, including basics like nickel and brass.

Sizes   Five sizes, from a tiny 00-bladed version to a size 5, 65mm long, 10g weight.

Use   This fast-sinking spinner is best suited to deeper or faster-flowing water. The deep, narrow blade on this spinner produces good vibration, and can be fished at a fairly fast retrieve without planing up.

Ultra Spinner   *PLATE C*

Manufacturer   Abu Garcia, UK

Classification   Spinner

Construction   Sonic blade, bomb-shaped body, fly-dressed treble hook.

Colours/finish   Four colours. Leaf-painted design on copper, silver or black blades.

Sizes   Available in 6g, 8g and 12g sizes.

Use   The off-centre blade creates sonic vibrations. Again, a small all-round spinner suitable for perch, chub and trout.

Veltic   *PLATE P*

Manufacturer   Rublex, France

Classification   Spinner

Construction   Rounded willow blade, heavy, brass fluted body, treble hook attached with a paper-clip type system. The treble comes with a red plastic tube covering the shank which slides over the 'paper clip' to immobilize it.

Colours/finish   Gold or Silver blade with distinctive, wavy black or red lines.

Sizes   Six sizes: 2g, 3.5g, 5g, 8g, 10g, 12g in weight.

Use   A traditional spinner which seems to have been around for ever. The blade's shape is somewhere between a French blade and a willow, and provides the lure with a very strong vibration. The smaller sizes are good for perch; go for the big ones for pike or large game fish. Less widely available than they used to be, but still in production and worth looking out for.

Voblex   *PLATE P*

Manufacturer   Rublex, France

Classification   Weight-forward spinner

Construction   Distinctive, hand-painted, offset hard rubber head with a painted fish eye mounted on a central wire shaft, just forward of an unusual, almost triangular, double-curved blade attached with a clevis. Small treble; shank dressed with red plastic tube.

Colours/finish   Available with Gold or Silver blade.

Sizes   Five sizes: 4g, 6g, 8g, 10g, and 12g.

Use   This old, reliable standby features in many tackle boxes. The offset rubber head helps prevent line twist and gives the spinner a fishy look as it moves through the water. Generally used as a shallow runner, the Voblex is a good all-round spinner, ideal for the beginner. Production problems during 1992 and '93 have made this lure more difficult to find in the shops than usual, but worth a hunt. Attractive to all species – the French use it especially for pike, perch and zander.

CHAPTER NINE
SPOONS

Spoons, as their name implies, are similar in design to the household spoon. Shapes, finishes and colours are available in virtually limitless numbers, but the basic design of a slightly convex piece of spoon-shaped metal with a hook attached at one end and a swivel or split ring at the other is fairly standard.

Spoons are not intended to revolve or spin like a spinner. They can therefore be fished much slower, since even when you stop reeling, most spoons will flutter to the bottom with at least some kind of action. Spoons are the basic winter standby for lure fishing in the UK, when most predatory fish are behaving quite sluggishly and are not in the mood for chasing around after their food.

Arrowhead Spoon PLATE A

Manufacturer   Rebel, USA

Classification   Spoon

Construction   An elongated, diamond-shaped spoon, featuring a heavy-duty, round bend treble hook, dressed with a red plastic tag and attached with a split ring. Supplied with a lightweight snap which should immediately be replaced before using in UK waters.

Colours/finish   Three finishes: silver plated, gold plated, black.

Sizes   One size: 57mm long, 14g weight.

Use   A variation on the spoon theme, this unusual-shaped spoon has a nice, tight wobble and a quality finish. Fish from the surface down to 10ft – useful for winter pike fishing, when more conventional spoons aren't producing.

Atlantic Spoon PLATE B

Manufacturer   Gordon Griffiths, UK

Classification   Spoon

Construction   Conventional Jim Vincent-shaped spoon, quality treble hook and swivel.

Colours/finish   Available in 12 colours and finishes, including hammered metal. Covers all the standard colours – copper/silver, hammered gold, hammered black and gold – plus some bright fluorescent colour schemes.

Sizes   Four basic sizes: 38mm, 7g weight; 51mm long, 11g weight; 63mm long, 14g weight; 89mm long, 28g weight, with heavy trolling versions of the three biggest sizes.

Use   The Atlantic is a very popular example of one of our most common lure designs. Works well retrieved erratically, slowly, slowly along the bottom. This makes it a highly effective cold water lure for pike, when the fish are at their most sluggish.

Others to try   Dardevle (Eppinger, USA).

Atom
PLATE B

Manufacturer Abu Garcia, UK

Classification Spoon

Construction Tapered rectangular-shaped blade with 'reflex ridges'. Atom has a second front-mounted treble, actually moulded on the front split ring (definitely a risk of tangles here!). Removing the front hook does not significantly alter the Atom's action.

Colours/finish Nine colours – Fire Orange and Green/Gold scale are particularly good.

Sizes Available in 12g, 20g, 25g, 35g weights.

Use A good, big water spoon, tried and tested over many years. One of the UK's best known and most popular pike lures, at its best in deeper water.

Others to try **Atom Giller** (Abu Garcia, UK). Weedless version.

Attractor
PLATE A

Manufacturer Lucky Strike, Canada

Classification Spoon

Construction Narrow, curved spoon with bubbled finish. Multifaceted red plastic bead inset in a copper wire threaded into the head. Two small flippers attached with split rings at tail; treble hook.

Colours/finish Six colour schemes, consisting of a diagonal fluorescent flash on a hammered nickel base. Red is favoured for fresh water, blue and yellow for sea work.

Sizes One size: 80mm long, 14g weight.

Use This spoon has a track record of catching big trout and salmon in Canada. With its combination of fluttering flippers, winking red eye, light-diffusing dimple finish and fluorescent flash pattern, combined with its tight, wobbling action, it seems to have almost too much to offer. Primarily designed as a game fish lure, it's an interesting one to use for pike, and even for the sea.

Banshee
PLATE A

Manufacturer Lucky Strike, Canada

Classification Spoon

Construction Shaped like a curved fish; treble hook with small flipper.

Colours/finish Four colours: Nickel, Gold, Pearl/Red, Fluorescent Yellow/Red.

Sizes One size: 55mm long, 5.5g weight.

Use This little lure has been around for some 60 years, and it's a favourite in Canada for trout. The action is very wild and erratic, twisting and weaving through the water. Its shape and light weight mean it doesn't cast very far, so it's best thought of as a short-range, small water spoon. Apart from trout, it will be taken by perch and (very readily) by pike, so watch out if you're using light tackle.

Beaded Back
PLATE A

Manufacturer Lucky Strike, Canada

Classification Spoon

Construction Narrow, oval-shaped spoon, gently curved. A slot runs along over half its length, enclosing five multifaceted red plastic beads threaded on copper wire. Treble hook.

Colours/finish   Two finishes: Gold and Nickel.

Sizes   One size: 85mm long, 14g weight.

Use   An interesting variant on the spoon theme. The water moving through the central slot creates a wake which, in addition to the side-to-side wobble and the flashing appearance of the beads, attracts hunting fish to investigate. Used in Canada for game fish, it's an alternative to try when more conventional patterns don't seem to be working.

Canoe   *PLATE A*

Manufacturer   Lucky Strike, Canada.

Classification   Spoon

Construction   The distinctive, long, slim-hollowed shape of this lure gives it its name. Treble hook.

Colours/finish   Some 12 colours; the best are probably the traditional Gold, Brass, Nickel and Pearl/Red.

Sizes   Two sizes: 165mm long, 50g weight; 120mm long, 28g weight.

Use   A big wobbling spoon with a rolling action, designed to attract big fish on the Canadian Lakes. The smaller version can be cast, the larger version is best suited for trolling the big lochs for salmon, pike and ferox and for sea work. Experience with this spoon in the UK is limited as yet.

Catcher   *PLATE B*

Manufacturer   Kilty, Ireland

Classification   Spoon

Construction   Very slimline spoon made from heavy gauge metal; heavy for its size. Treble hook.

Colours/finish   Available in Gold, Silver and Copper, plus a variety of prismatic finishes.

Sizes   Two sizes offered: 75mm and 95mm, 16g and 22g weight.

Use   Catcher has a great reputation as an estuary lure for sea trout and salmon; it's also a super sea lure for all species. This lure will catch mackerel, gar fish along the surface, bass, pollack and even cod. Probably less used for pike except in fast or deep river situations, where its weight will keep it close to the bottom.

Sadly, this popular lure is likely to become a victim of the lure manufacturers' curious enthusiasm for discontinuing popular lures. Soon, it may well follow Lucky 13, Gudebrod Sniper, River Runt and many others into the Great Snag in the Lake – lure collectors please note!

Cisco   *PLATE A*

Manufacturer   Lindquist Bait Co, Canada

Classification   Spoon

Construction   This is an unusual-shaped spoon with asymmetric stubby 'fins' and a particularly large, pierced attachment point at the head, allowing very free movement of the lure. Positions for optional hook attachment on the ends of each fin. Good treble hook.

Colours/finish   Available in 12 colours, from Chrome to Frog, with a range of simple, bright painted patterns; the Chartreuse/ Fluorescent Green version has won a lot of favour in the UK. The bright red version, which proved very successful for deep loch piking, is unfortunately no longer available, but the orange, red and black version seems to be proving itself a good substitute.

Sizes   The Cisco comes in four sizes, the two larger (133mm and 82mm, weights 28g and 42g) being the most popular in the UK.

Use   The Cisco is a lure much used by pike anglers for both bank and trolling methods. Its flickering, darting roll gives the Cisco a unique action which works well at slow and fast trolling speeds and, as many UK anglers have discovered, also acts effectively for bank fishing. A sink-and-draw type retrieve has proved effective, as the Cisco flutters very alluringly on the sink phase. (Don't confuse this with the Cisco Kid, which is a floating diving plug.)

Dardevle   *PLATE A*

Manufacturer   Eppinger, USA

Classification   Spoon

Construction   Narrow, medium-thickness spoon with a heavy-duty treble.

Colours/finish   A range of 29 colours is available, the best and most famous of which is the classic red and white version. American and Canadian Flag models are available for those who like something different, and a good choice of more serious options is on offer. Genuine Dardevles have the little devil's head trademark stamped on the convex side.

Sizes   Just one size for the spoon bearing the name Dardevle: 90mm long, 28g weight, but there are some 50-odd variations on this spoon, from the tiny Dardevle Skeeter weighing less than a gram to the giant Huskie Devle weighing 91g.

Use   The Dardevle (pronounced 'dare-devil') has been around for over 80 years. Named in honour of American flying aces, this is probably the most famous and the most imitated spoon in the world. Perfectly balanced to fish at any speed, the best known application is the red and white spoon fished fast for pike – very effective.

Derrick Amies Norfolk Spoon
PLATE B

Manufacturer   Bettell Lures, UK

Classification   Spoon

Construction   A Jim Vincent modelled spoon, hand-made, with a highly polished finish. Spoons are hand-stamped 'Derrick Amies Norfolk Spoon'.

Colours/finish   Offered in Copper, Copper/Silver, Brass and Brass/Silver.

Sizes   Available in two sizes: 130 × 35mm and 100 × 30mm, weights 28g and 18g.

Use   A classy spoon, hand-made by the inimitable Charlie Bettell. Charlie would decline to be called an expert, but anybody purchasing any of his beautifully made lures (*See* Appendix A) might well want to argue with him about that. These spoons are superb in the shallowish waters of the Norfolk Broads, for which they were designed. For deeper water fishing, add a barrel or Wye lead to give extra casting distance. Fish them low and slow for winter pike. A future collector's item for sure.

Devil   *PLATE B*

Manufacturer   Intrepid, UK

Classification   Spoon

Construction Conventional spoon, Mustad treble, medium-thickness metal.

Colours/finish Red/White only.

Sizes Three sizes: 7g, 12g and 18g weight.

Use A good casting lure for its size – use a medium-speed retrieve with the occasional burst of speed. Imitation is, of course, the sincerest form of flattery, and this is one of many spoons which pays homage to the 80-year-plus history of the Dardevle spoon. Widely available.

Doctor Spoon
PLATE A

Manufacturer Arbogast, USA

Classification Spoon

Construction Solid brass, fish-shaped spoon, said to be the original version of this style of lure. Equipped with a heavy-duty treble hook which can be attached via a split ring to either end.

Colours/finish A huge range of 53 versions, based mainly on chrome, gold, copper, green, white, yellow and black backgrounds, with various colour-reflective flashes. The classic Copper and Chrome/Gold are probably the ones to go for.

Sizes Five sizes: 32mm long, 5.25g weight (Midget Doctor); 48mm long, 7g weight (Spin Doctor); 57mm long, 10.5g weight (Baby Doctor); 83mm long, 17.5g weight ('Little Doc'); 114mm long, 33g weight ('Big Doc').

Use A wide, side-to-side wobble and a tempting flutter on the drop make this a very effective spoon for pike and trout. It's also popular in the US for walleye (zander). A little heavier for its size than the very similar Pro-

fessor. The much lighter Thin Doctor version is a very good trolling spoon.

Others to try Professor (Kuusamo, Finland).

Effzett
PLATE B

Manufacturer D.A.M., UK

Classification Spoon

Construction Almost oblong-shaped, and heavy for its size. The convex size has a scaled finish. Single treble hook (except for the largest size, which has a second treble attached to the swivel), good quality fittings, red tag.

Colours/finish Nine colours including Silver, Copper and Gold, the others being variations on these.

Sizes Five sizes: 32mm long, 6g weight; 45mm long, 16g weight; 55mm long, 22g weight; 65mm long, 30g weight; 80mm long, 45g weight.

Use A classic-style spoon which is useful for all predator-fishing in open water. Its size-to-weight ratio makes it useful for casting into the wind. Very popular in Europe, where it sells in large numbers.

Favourite Vass
PLATE B

Manufacturer Abu Garcia, UK

Classification Spoon

Construction A weedless spoon, with a large single hook protected by a twin pronged weed guard. The hook is dressed with a bucktail.

Colours/finish Six colours. Black/Gold and plain Gold are popular.

Sizes Available in just one size, 15g.

Use This spoon has been around for a few years now, and it's useful when fishing in weedy areas, casting it into clear areas and bringing it back through weed on the retrieve. Don't forget to bend the weed guard prongs back out past the hook, otherwise it won't be weedless! Widely available.

Others to try **Lucky Strike Weedless** (Lucky Strike, Canada).

Half Wave
PLATE A

Manufacturer Lucky Strike, Canada

Classification Spoon

Construction A fairly wide spoon, one side of which is crimped along its length to produce a wave effect. Heavy-duty treble.

Colours/finish Two colours, Gold/Red/White, Nickel/Red/White.

Sizes Five sizes: from 38mm long, 5g weight, to 115mm long, 35g weight.

Use A good, meaty spoon with a well balanced wobbling action. Watch the speed of retrieve with this one; too fast and you'll lose all action. Hard to say what effect those crimpy waves have, but they will almost certainly set up a slightly different pattern of vibration than a lure of similar pattern without them. Try bumping this slowly along the bottom in winter, to stir up torpid pike. A very big-selling spoon in Canada.

Ham Spoon (aka **White Water Spoon**)
PLATE B

Manufacturer Gordon Griffiths, UK

Classification Spoon

Construction Dumpy-bodied, fat pear-shaped spoon, making the lure heavy for its size. Treble hook.

Colours/finish Hammered and plain finishes in Gold, Silver and Copper.

Sizes Three sizes: 30mm, 37mm and 43mm long, 7g, 14g, and 18g weight.

Use As the name White Water Spoon suggests, this spoon is ideal for use in fast-flowing rivers, where its size-to-weight ratio helps get it down to where the fish are. With its vigorous action, it's ideal for salmon, sea trout and trout.

Hawaiian Spoon
PLATE A

Manufacturer Arbogast, USA

Classification Weedless spoon

Construction A fish-shaped spoon with an integral hook, weed guard and removable skirt. The spoon body is a solid lead alloy casting, giving very good casting ability.

Colours/finish Comes in seven colour schemes: Black, Scale, Yellow, Shad, Coach Dog, Black Stripe and Red Stripe.

Sizes Two sizes: 7g and 11g.

Use This is a useful lure for heavily weeded areas, although lighter, weedless spoons might be better if weed cover is really dense. Because of its weight, this lure needs a fairly rapid retrieve, accompanied by a strong lift of the rod tip. Fish frequently hit this lure on the drop, so make sure line tension is maintained. It would be an interesting choice to troll around deep water obstructions, rocks, etc.

Others to try **Jaw-Breaker** (Northland, USA).

Heron   *PLATE B*

Manufacturer   Kilty, Ireland

Classification   Spoon

Construction   Long, tapering 'shoe-horn'-shaped spoon, VMC treble.

Colours/finish   Available in Gold, Copper, Silver and a variety of superb enamelled paint finishes. Copper and Silver are very effective.

Sizes   Sizes range from 30g up to a mighty 100g, measuring a full 178mm long.

Use   This is one of the biggest spoons currently available. Its traditional body shape in a variety of weights and lengths makes this a versatile big water lure. The Heron is really designed as a trolling lure, but in its lighter weights will find some uses for shorter-range work on fen drains, etc. Heron is another lure which sadly looks as if it may be on its way out, despite being a standard lure much favoured by the 'trout water' pike enthusiasts.

Others to try   The larger **Professors** (Kuusamo, Finland).

Herri   *PLATE B*

Manufacturer   Landa Sports, UK

Classification   Spoon

Construction   A thin profile, heavy-metal elongated spoon with a red plastic tail flipper, quality treble and swivel.

Colours/finish   Five top-performing sea colours: Gold, Copper, Silver, Silver/Blue and Mackerel.

Sizes   Six sizes: from 6g to 30g weight.

Use   Fish patterns and sparkling prism effects make these look very lifelike in the water. Long-casting, especially in the heavier weights. A good sea lure, both for shore work or for pier fishing for summertime mackerel and garfish. The Herri is also handy for deeper-water cod, pollack and bass.

Others to try   Also available with a front-mounted rotating blade, when it's known as the Herri+Flipz.

Huskie Devle Junior   *PLATE A*

Manufacturer   Eppinger, USA

Classification   Trolling spoon

Construction   Broad, medium-thickness spoon, treble hook.

Colours/finish   Some 27 colours, including the classic Red/White, Yellow with Red Diamonds and, of course, the standard metallic finishes.

Sizes   One size: 115mm long, 56g weight.

Use   Specifically designed as a heavy spoon for slow trolling in deep water, for salmon, lake trout, muskie and pike. In the UK, it comes into its own on the lochs and big reservoirs. Like all Eppinger lures, it's well made and well balanced. Not suitable for casting any distance.

Others to try Comes in an even bigger **Huskie Devle** version at 91g.

Jawbreaker   *PLATE A*

Manufacturer Northland, USA

Classification Weedless spoon

Construction Small spoon with a weighted stainless-steel single hook, a Y-shaped plastic weed guard and rubber skirt. Reflective decal on convex face.

Colours/finish Twelve colours with complementary skirts; Chartreuse Sunrise (yellow and orange) is popular.

Sizes One size: 55mm long, 14g weight.

Use Claimed to be totally weedless, this lure is designed to fish through topwater, over lily pads and around weed beds, attracting fish waiting in cover. Fished at slow to moderate speed, it has a very lively slithering wobbling action. Twitching the rod tip produces a life-like swimming look, especially at slow speeds. This spoon can also be bumped along the bottom during winter months, with very little fear of getting caught up. Easy to fish on either top or bottom.

Others to try **Weedless** (Lucky Strike, Canada).

Kerryman   *PLATE B*

Manufacturer Kilty, Ireland

Classification Spoon

Construction Streamline spoon with a slight ridge and 'S' profile, large reflective eye. Treble hook.

Colours/finish Available in Gold, Silver, Copper/Silver and Copper.

Sizes Offered in three sizes: 14g, 18g and 22g.

Use A very long-casting spoon, suitable for casting into the wind, which has a good slow roll. Something of a banker, the Kerryman often delivers when other lures are drawing blanks. Suitable for all predators, and fishes particularly well sink-and-draw style in winter.

Koster   *PLATE B*

Manufacturer Abu, UK

Classification Spoon

Construction Slim, heavyweight spoon, ridged back, good quality treble, but cheap looking swivel.

Colours/finish Silver, Silver/Red, Silver/Blue.

Sizes Three sizes: 18g, 28g, 40g weight.

Use A popular, heavy salmon spoon for deep, fast-water conditions. Also finds favour amongst sea anglers for long casting for mackerel shoals and bass. The 40g version on a carp rod can be cast well over 100 yards.

Kraut   *PLATE B*

Manufacturer D.A.M., UK

Classification Weedless spoon

Construction Based on the Effzett spoon, but with fixed double hook, weed guards and feather dressing. Quality swivel.

Colours/finish   Just one colour: silver with a red stripe, dressed with red and yellow feathers.

Sizes   Four sizes; 32mm long, 6g weight; 45mm long, 16g weight; 55mm long, 22g weight; 65mm long, 30g weight.

Use   Useful in snaggy or weedy waters, where you might have problems in using a conventional treble. (The term 'weedless' in relative of course – you can still get snagged up, but it's less likely when a lure has weed guards.) Try running the Kraut along the bottom to stir up somnolent mid-season pike, or wobbling it slowly alongside a weed bed.

Krocodile   *PLATE A*

Manufacturer   Luhr-Jensen, USA

Classification   Spoon

Construction   A narrow 'shoehorn'-shaped spoon, made from solid brass. Available in treble hook, double hook, bucktail treble, bucktail single and single tube tail versions.

Colours/finish   Comes in 56 finishes, ranging from basic brass and chrome to exotics like lime green fish scale and metallic perch. Not all versions are available in all colours, and the choice is much more limited in the larger sizes.

Sizes   There are 18 size/weight combinations, ranging from a dinky 32mm long, 4.6g weight to a very substantial 155mm long, 196g weight trolling version.

Use   Owing to its compactness, this is a long-casting, fast-sinking spoon, with a tight, violent, erratic-wobbling action. Can be cast, jigged or trolled – with a downrigger, in deeper water. The action of this lure would

attract any predator; the larger sizes are particularly suitable for saltwater use.

Krokodil   *PLATE B*

Manufacturer   Bete, Finland

Classification   Spoon

Construction   Leaf-shaped spoon, with a centrally attached, revolving red multi-faceted 'eye' bead. The treble hook has a leaf-shaped plastic fin attached. Front split ring and swivel.

Colours/finish   A range of 20 colours: a good Black/Gold, somewhat insipid Perch, three super spotted ones and some interesting Herringbones.

Sizes   Four sizes: 45mm long, 10g weight; 60mm long, 12g weight; 70mm long, 18g weight; 80mm long, 23g weight.

Use   An attractive, good quality general-purpose spoon, which casts well for its size. A medium-depth spoon, with a good record as a game lure, on account of some nice salmon and sea trout colour schemes.

Lizard   *PLATE A*

Manufacturer   Lucky Strike, Canada

Classification   Spoon

Construction   Thin blade, slightly S-shaped profile with a slight ridge along its length. Treble hook; small, red plastic flipper.

Colours/finish   Some 15 colours: Nickel, Gold and Red/White are probably the first ones to go for, and of these, Nickel is thought the best.

Sizes Two sizes: 80mm long, 18g weight; 110mm long, 28g weight.

Use A well balanced spoon with a nice fluttering action, which maintains stability when fished slowly. This is regarded as an absolute must for pike by those UK anglers who have tried it. Because of its relative thinness, it works well at slow speeds and sinks slowly, making it ideal for winter work in shallow water, when slow lures are needed to attract inactive fish.

Lukki   *PLATE B*

Manufacturer Landa Sports, UK

Classification Spoon

Construction Thin profile, beautiful quality enamelled style finish, with fins shaped for a swimming action, quality treble hook and swivel.

Colours/finish Nine colours are offered, all of which look very enticing, the Brown Trout and Rainbow Trout are particularly good looking.

Sizes Seven sizes, from 7g to 28g in weight.

Use This is a very familiar lure, widely distributed in tackle shops, and it's a good one to look out for if you need a long casting spoon to use in fast-flowing water. It produces a good swimming action, will work well at depth, and is suitable for salmon, sea trout, pike – most species, in fact.

Others to try Also available with a front-mounted rotating blade – the **Lukki+Flipz**, and in the **Lukki Turbo** version (both by Landa Sports, UK).

Lukki Turbo   *PLATE B*

Manufacturer Landa Sports, UK

Classification Spoon

Construction A narrow-bladed finned spoon of unusual design, with three horizontal slits cut in the lure body and a quality hook and swivel.

Colours/finish Comes in eight colours, including a very attractive Brown Trout and the equally good Silver Pearl.

Sizes Available in two sizes: 18g and 24g weight.

Use This spoon produces a good vibration, as the water flows turbulently through the slits in the lure as it's retrieved. This creates additional noise and vibration in the water, enhancing its fish-attracting properties. This is a very unusual design, and certainly one to try if you are fishing in deep, fast water and want to show the fish something different.

Miki   *PLATE B*

Manufacturer Kilty, Eire

Classification Spoon

Construction Big, wide-bodied spoon. The fish 'eye' gives an extra feature to this classy lure. Good treble hook.

Colours/finish Available in Gold, Silver and Copper as well as a range of high-quality painted finishes, including Roach, Bream, Perch and Mackerel.

Sizes Three sizes: 76mm long, 18g weight; 83mm long, 32g weight; 83mm long, 42g weight.

Use The Miki is a big-water spoon suitable for either trolling or long casting. The 42g version, in particular, can be cast very long distances indeed. Suitable for pike and lough trout and salmon. Also useful in sea fishing, where a heavy lure is needed. The Miki has also gone on a few mahseer expeditions recently, with some success.

Others to try **Equalizer** (Shakespeare, UK), not to be confused with **Equalizer** (Magna Strike, USA), which is a diving plug.

Nix
PLATE B

Manufacturer Bete, Finland

Classification Weedless spoon

Construction Rounded, rectangular-shaped chunky spoon. Armed with a double hook which is fixed by a rivet to the high gloss blade. The hook is protected by a sprung wire, two-pronged weed guard. Split ring and swivel.

Colours/finish Some 20 colours available, the same range as for the Krokodil.

Sizes Three sizes: 50mm long, 9g weight; 62mm long, 16g weight; 75mm long, 23g weight.

Use A useful semi-weedless spoon for skittering through top water in summer or crawling carefully along the bottom in winter. Make sure the weedless prongs are proud of the hook, or it won't be weedless at all!

Pikko
PLATE B

Manufacturer Landa Sports, UK

Classification Spoon

Construction Conventional, broad-bladed, egg-shaped spoon finished in excellent quality baked-on colour finish. Plastic tail flipper, quality treble and swivel.

Colours/finish Five colours, including a super pike design, Yellow Perch, Golden Rudd and Silver Dace.

Sizes Seven sizes: from 12g to 25g.

Use This is primarily a pike lure, but it also boasts a good track record for salmon and lake trout, too. In the smaller sizes, expect this spoon to be taken by perch and small trout. The Pikko has a nice, lazy, rolling action. This is a quality spoon, widely distributed in the UK.

Professor
PLATE B

Manufacturer Kuusamo, Finland

Classification Spoon

Construction A fish-shaped spoon which is designed for the trace to be attached at either end. Treble hooks are mounted at either end of the elongated body; the unused treble should be removed before fishing, to avoid tangles. The whole range (except for the 00) is available with or without a red rotating bead eye, built into the spoon body. Sizes 2 and 3 are available in weedless format with a weedless treble; sizes 2, 3, and 4 are available in scale finishes.

Colours/finish A series of fairly unimaginative finishes: Copper, Nickel/Brass, Blue Perch, Nickel/Copper, Black Perch, Redbelly, plus a newly available Red/Blue combination. Not all sizes are available in all colours.

Sizes Available in five sizes from the 8g mini version up to the 60g, 200mm long trolling version. Size 1 (27g) is the most popular size for pike, although the mega trolling version is one of the standard big winter spoons today.

Use Fished 'eye' end up the line, the lure fishes with a fast roll, giving a repeating flash. With the blunt end up the line, a much slower wobble results. Try stopping the retrieve and you will see that the Professor sinks back at an angle with an attractive flutter. Highly recommended for trolling, and in the smaller sizes for deep water lakes, pits and reservoirs. A favourite in the UK.

Others to try Doctor Spoon (Arbogast, USA).

Red Flash   *PLATE A*

Manufacturer Lucky Strike, Canada

Classification Spoon

Construction Pointed, oval-shaped spoon with two large faceted red plastic beads threaded on a copper wire and inset into the spoon. Treble hook.

Colours/finish Two colours: Gold and Nickel.

Sizes Two sizes: 89mm long and 74mm long, 20g weight.

Use A good wobbling action coupled with the visual and sonic attraction of the lurid red 'eyes' make this an effective spoon for pike and trout. In Canada, it's used for big lake trout and muskies (the latter are notoriously hard to catch). Something different to try when more conventional patterns don't seem to be working.

Rex Spoon   *PLATE A*

Manufacturer Weezel Bait Co, USA

Classification Weedless spoon

Construction Stamped brass or stainless steel, wire weed guard (except on 28g size), hand-tied hackle feather tail. Single fixed hook (on the 14g and 28g sizes this is secured with a brass plated screw for easy replacement). The 28g size comes with an extra trailer hook.

Colours/finish Four colours: Chrome, Gold, Black and Copper, with a choice of six colours of tail feathers.

Sizes Four sizes: 1.5g, 7g, 14g and 28g weight.

Use In production since 1941, the Rex Spoon has an honourable history. It was included in the US Forces Survival Kit during World War II, testament to its fish-catching abilities in the most dire of circumstances, and is used as a pattern for this purpose right up to date. It has a good darting action, and a fast rocking wobble; the feathers add extra interest. Suitable for pike, perch, salmon trout, and sea species; sea anglers will be particularly interested in the 28g stainless-steel version.

Scarlet Eye   *PLATE A*

Manufacturer Lucky Strike, Canada

Classification Spoon

Construction A roughly S-shaped profile with a round scooped head, giving the general impression of a fish shape. Enclosed in the head is a multi-faceted red plastic bead. Treble hook.

101

Colours/finish Two finishes: Nickel and Gold.

Sizes Three sizes: 44mm, 76mm and 102mm long, 15g, 18g and 25g weights.

Use An unusually shaped spoon with a side-to-side wobbling action. The red bead rotates as the lure is retrieved, creating bubbles and noise. It can be fished very high in the water, and seems to work best in warm water, when the fish want something to chase. Experiment with speed of retrieve – the action is not very tolerant of being fished too fast or too slow.

Smakk   *PLATE B*

Manufacturer Intrepid, UK

Classification Spoon

Construction Lightweight, pressed metal Toby-style spoon. Red-painted rear fin, scale finish. Mustad treble.

Colours/finish Silver only.

Sizes Four sizes: 7g, 12g, 18g, 28g weight.

Use Primarily intended as a long-casting lure for deep, heavy water – go for the largest size for this kind of application. Tobys spin rather than wobble, so make certain you have a good swivel somewhere in your set-up. Widely available.

Sonic   *PLATE B*

Manufacturer Kilty, Ireland

Classification Spoon

Construction Essentially a smaller, slimmer version of the Miki (made from heavier gauge metal). Consequently, weight for weight, the Sonic even outcasts the Miki! Good treble hook.

Colours/finish Available in the same range of colours as the Miki – Perch and Mackerel are particularly liked.

Sizes Comes in two sizes: 22g and 28g weight, both 76mm long.

Use The Sonic is a superb general-purpose spoon for big lakes, rivers and reservoirs, where fish are likely to be taken at some depth. Primarily a pike lure, it has found favour amongst big-water game anglers, and has also been used for rock fishing for bass and pollack.

Southport Slammer   *PLATE A*

Manufacturer Rebel, USA

Classification Spoon

Construction Stainless-steel slim spoon, with 3X treble attached with a stainless-steel split ring.

Colours/finish Comes in real silver plate, real gold plate and a silver G-Finish. Each spoon comes packed with three strips of brightly coloured prismatic Mylar Tape, so that the spoon can be customized to suit your fancy.

Sizes One size: 83mm long, 10.5g weight.

Use This is a trolling spoon; the action varies according to the speed at which you fish it – from a slow, rolling wobble to a wild flashing frenzy. Designed for the Great Lakes, where it is used for salmon, steelhead, brown trout and lake trout, valuable here for sea work, pike and ferox.

Squid Spoon   *PLATE A*

Manufacturer   Homemade

Classification   Spoon

Construction   Made from an old dessert spoon with the handle cut off and the end smoothed, Sampo split rings, stainless-steel swivel, Partridge Grey Shadow treble and a plastic squid found idling around in the bottom of a tackle box.

Colours/finish   Anything you can dream up.

Sizes   Once again, more or less anything you want; this one weighs 25g and measures 65mm long.

Use   A medium-thick spoon which casts over the horizon and produces a sliding wobble. Bashing with a round-ended hammer would produce a thinner spoon with a more fluttering action. This spoon has been given good quality fittings. The whole thing cost hardly anything, including the spoon itself (bought as part of a job lot at a car boot sale). If you decided to use cheaper fittings and a few feathers or some red wool instead of a squid, the cost would be halved. Unless you are very skilled, it's hard to make homemade spoons which will consistently produce a quality, balanced action. They come into their own, though, for exploring snaggy swims, where the possible sacrifice of your expensive shop-bought favourites comes hard on the pocket.

Stor-Oringen (aka **Big Wiggley**)   *PLATE B*

Manufacturer   Abu Garcia, UK

Classification   Spoon

Construction   Curved, wide 'shoe-horn'-shaped spoon, single treble attached with split ring, painted one side, plastic tail tag.

Colours/finish   Good quality baked-on finish; comes in several strong colours, including unusual red or yellow with black bars.

Sizes   Three sizes: 15g, 20g and 25g weight.

Use   This spoon casts well, and has an attractive slow wobble. Another variation on the quality spoon theme, recommended by the manufacturer for pike, zander and trout – one to choose for reservoir fish.

Syclops   *PLATE A*

Manufacturer   Mepps, France

Classification   Spoon

Construction   Ridge back slim spoon, scale finish, treble hook, plastic grub tail (also available without the tail).

Colours/finish   Available in gold, silver, black and four eye-jolting fluorescent colours.

Sizes   Five sizes offered, from 5g to 26g.

Use   An interesting spoon variant. The fluorescent colours are claimed to have superior visibility at depth and under poor light conditions, and the large size in fluorescent green or orange are well liked for sea work. Good general-purpose spoon for all predators. Another high performance lure from the Mepps stable; fairly widely available.

Tiger   *PLATE B*

Manufacturer   Intrepid, UK

Classification   Spoon

Spoons

Construction 'Atom'-style spoon, chunky size, with a scale finish and a plastic fin tag. The plated hook on the example shown in plate B showed signs of corrosion whilst still in the blister pack.

Colours/finish Silver only.

Sizes Two sizes: 16g and 22g.

Use A widely available, low-cost spoon, which does not have the finesse of some of the better known (and more expensive) spoons we list here, but will nevertheless catch plenty of fish. One to reserve for exploring snaggy areas, perhaps?

Timber Doodle *PLATE B*

Manufacturer Mepps, France

Classification Spoon

Construction A weedless spoon, the hook being integral with the spoon body. A front-mounting pin allows a soft plastic twin-tailed worm to be mounted.

Colours/finish Available in Gold Silver and Black spoon colours, with Pumpkin, White and Chartreuse worms.

Sizes Two sizes offered: 8g and 12g weight.

Use This spoon is specifically designed for fishing in and around weed beds and snaggy areas. It has an erratic fluttering action, enhanced by the scrumptious looking worm which wiggles behind it. A good caster, this is a highly rated spoon for pike, perch and zander in Europe.

Others to try **Jaw-Breaker** (Northland, USA).

Toby *PLATE B*

Manufacturer Abu Garcia, UK

Classification Spoon

Construction Elongated fish-shaped body, complete with rear fins, scale finish, nice big eye. The sensible-sized hooks are well in proportion to the lure's size.

Colours/finish Seven colours, from the traditional gold and silver through baked-on bright greens and reds to the ever popular black with gold bars.

Sizes Toby is available in 7g, 10g, 12g, 18g, 20g, 28g weights.

Use The Toby is one of the best known salmon and sea trout lures, and has been for many years – most lure boxes will contain a Toby or two. It combines an excellent rolling action with good, long-casting performance. Especially recommended in fast water. Also has its devotees amongst sea anglers and pike anglers.

Others to try **Toby Sulmo** (bright colour schemes).
Toby Tiger (fluorescent colours).
Toby Trolling (silver-striped patterns).
Toby Vass (weedless version).
(All produced by Abu Garcia, UK.)

Trophy II *PLATE A*

Manufacturer Williams, Canada

Classification Spoon

Construction Fat, oval-shaped spoon, with a stabilizing ridge along part of the length and a VMC cone-cut treble hook.

104

Colours/finish Six options: a plain silver plated version plus five with reflective decals.

Sizes One size: 63mm long, 21g weight.

Use Use for casting or trolling with a slow-to-medium retrieve. The fluttering action displays plenty of flash, and is also good on the drop. Designed for game fish, this lure was introduced in 1993 and so has not been used extensively in the UK, but it's a good quality version of a relatively uncommon style of spoon.

Turku   *PLATE B*

Manufacturer Nils Master, Finland

Classification Spoon

Construction Oval-shaped medium-thickness spoon, painted eye, treble hook, red plastic flipper.

Colours/finish A range of 20 colours, with a good choice of classic metal finishes, spot, stripe and scale combinations.

Sizes One size: 90mm long, 33g weight.

Use A good quality all-purpose spoon, easy to cast, this is a fast sinker for use in medium to deep fast-flowing water. Use a medium retrieve with occasional sharp jerks, giving the appearance of a wounded fish. Suitable for all predators.

Uto   *PLATE B*

Manufacturer Abu Garcia, UK

Classification Spoon

Construction Rectangular-shaped blade

gives this lure a 'big' action. Has an additional front-mounted treble (beware of line becoming tangled on it). The rear treble has a plastic tail fin.

Colours/finish Available in six colours: Blue Scale in the larger sizes is popular, as is the Perch (a little wishy washy, in our opinion, but we tend to prefer strong colours).

Sizes Three sizes: 18g, 25g and 35g weight.

Use A big water lure, suitable for perch, pike and big lake trout. Needs a good depth of water to be at its most effective. Widely available. (Not to be confused with the Uto from Nils Master.)

Wabbler   *PLATE A*

Manufacturer Williams, Canada

Classification Spoon

Construction A light spoon with the distinctive Williams stabilizing ridge running down two-thirds of its length. Equipped with a VMC treble.

Colours/finish Fourteen finishes, all of which are based on 24k gold or pure silver-plated base colours. (Not all colours are available in junior and giant sizes.)

Sizes Five sizes: 38mm long, 7g weight (junior); 57mm long, 7g weight (small); 67mm long, 14g weight (medium); 82mm long, 21g weight (large); 101mm long, 28g weight (giant).

Use A thin, light spoon with a very pronounced wobble – so strong that care must be taken not to retrieve too fast, or the spoon will flip over and lose all its action – despite the stabilizing ridge, which seems less effective on this model. A good swivel is essential. Not particularly easy to cast into the wind, this spoon comes into its own when used for slow trolling with a downrigger.

Weedless Devil Bait   *PLATE A*

Manufacturer Lucky Strike, Canada

Classification Weedless spoon

Construction Slim spoon, slightly up-turned at the end, pierced to allow the positioning of a single fixed hook. Twin-pronged wire weed guard.

Colours/finish Six colours: Red/White, Nickel, Gold, Fluorescent Green, Fluorescent Orange, Yellow/Red Diamonds.

Sizes Three sizes: 60mm long, 9g weight; 80mm long, 18g weight; 40mm long, 5g weight.

Use With its slightly upturned lip, this lure can be made to ride high in the water and skid around surface obstructions. Use it like this in the summer, but remember to start your retrieve just as soon as the spoon hits the water, and to keep your rod tip up. Later in the year, take advantage of its fast-sinking and weed-avoiding properties and work it slowly along the bottom. As with all spoons of this construction, make sure the weed-guard prongs are covering the hook before casting.

Whitefish   *PLATE A*

Manufacturer Williams, Canada

Classification Spoon

Construction Long, slim spoon with a distinctive stabilizing ridge running down half the length of the lure. VMC treble.

Colours/finish These classy spoons are plated in 24k gold or pure silver. There are ten versions in all, including gold and silver wrinkled, half and half gold and silver, and four silver versions with a coloured flash.

Sizes Five sizes: 57mm long, 7g weight; 83mm long, 10.5g weight; 108mm long, 21g weight; 133mm long, 28g weight; 153mm long, 42g weight.

Use The stabilizing bar gives the Whitefish a good balanced action and enables it to be fished at quite shallow depths. Seems not to twist, even when retrieved at speed. The luxury finish sounds like a gimmick, but the highly reflective surfaces of precious metals have a lot to recommend them. An all-round spoon, suitable for freshwater and sea predators, used for game fish in Canada. The gold finish is said to be best for pike.

X-2 Rocket   *PLATE A*

Manufacturer Lucky Strike, Canada

Classification Spoon

Construction Toby-type lure with an S-profile, four small fins and a treble hook. Light fish-scale pattern.

Colours/finish Two finishes: nickel and gold, both with red fins.

Sizes Two sizes: 90mm long, 20g weight; 63mm long, 14g weight.

Use A classic spoon for salmon, trout and pike, and a good long caster, the action making it look like a flickering fish. Suitable for deep and fast-flowing water. Always fished with a swivel to avoid line twist; an over-fast retrieve results in loss of action; medium speed is best.

CHAPTER TEN
SPINNERBAITS

Spinnerbaits are amongst the least familiar of lures in the UK, and often prompt the question, 'Do they *really* catch fish?' The answer is a resounding 'Yes!', and many people rely on them as the chief part of their fishing armoury. The spinnerbait owes much of its reputation in the UK to Dr Barrie Rickards, who used these lures to deadly effect on the drains and dykes of East Anglia.

Spinnerbaits have a coathanger-shaped wire form, the upper arm with one or two spinner blades attached via a swivel, the lower with a jig head and a single hook, usually dressed with a skirt. Occasionally, there will be twin upper arms, each having a spinner blade. Like most spinners, there are many variations in blades, some having two types of blade to produce different vibration patterns.

As spinnerbaits have bodied hooks (known in the US as keel weighted), so the point of the hook is away from the river bottom. This makes spinnerbaits much less likely to snag weed, and so they can be used where other spinners cannot. When fishing a very snaggy swim, choose a version with heavier wire, which will be easier to get out of trouble. Otherwise, look for a lighter wire which will collapse easily when taken by a fish, thus improving hooking.

You'll see spinnerbaits referred to as having open or closed throats. Open throats have a simple angled bend for line attachment; closed-throat versions have the wire in a closed loop. If you are going to use a wire trace (and we regard this as essential for all lure fishing where pike are the target or may be present in the water), you should go for the closed-throat version, which will prevent your trace sliding up the arms of the lure. This does not matter where you are tying a lure directly on to your line, and open or closed throat versions can be selected. A valve rubber or a twist of wire can be used to make a quick conversion from open to closed, where needed.

Spinnerbaits with big wide blades kite up towards the surface on retrieve, and can be fished easily, quite fast, just underneath the surface. Fish more slowly, and the lure will run more deeply; as with all lure fishing, you need to experiment to find out what your lure can do.

These are not the best of lures for long-distance casting, due to their hopeless aerodynamics – they are at their best on narrow, shallowish, weedy waters and for fishing from boats.

———— ♦ ————

Arrow Spin   *PLATE D*

Manufacturer   Rebel, USA

Classification   Spinnerbait

Construction   Diamond-shaped spoon with a single hook, and a light wire arm with willow-leaf blade attached with a split ring.

Colours/finish   Silver plated, gold plated and black.

Sizes   One size: 57mm long, 14g weight.

Use Versatile and unusual hybrid lure, half-way between a spoon and a spinnerbait. Fish fast around weed beds, and it's quite resistant to snagging up. Cast it into holes and allow it to flutter down, almost using it like a jig. Alternatively, use it like a normal spinnerbait with a steady or sink-and-draw retrieve.

Big Bass   *PLATE D*

Manufacturer Blue Fox, USA

Classification Spinnerbait

Construction The tandem blade version has a large willow blade attached with a Sampo swivel, and a small Indiana Blade. Single 4/0 hook, closed throat, natural rubber quality skirt. The pack also includes a stinger hook, useful when fish are coming short.

Colours/finish Blades: Silver and Gold. Skirts: Chartreuse, Black, Yellow, Black/Chartreuse, Pumpkin Seed.

Sizes One size: 14g weight.

Use A good quality spinnerbait, fairly easily available in the UK. The single-bladed version, much lighter at 7g, is open throated, and so may need to be adapted with a valve rubber or piece of wire twisted around the neck. Designed for largemouth bass by Roland Martin, one of the top Lake Okeechobee (Florida) bass pros, but our fish like it too!

Bionic Bucktail   *PLATE D*

Manufacturer Northland, USA

Classification Spinnerbait

Construction Wire coathanger form, large jig head with painted eye, tandem blades (a small Colorado and a large willow), single hook dressed with natural bucktail and feather, trailing treble hook attached with a split ring.

Colours/finish Six colours: White, Yellow, Black, Green, Orange and Chartreuse Sunrise, all with added glitter on the blades.

Sizes One size: 170mm length (including trailer hook and dressing), 21g weight.

Use Designed specifically for casting and trolling for big fish – in particular for northern pike and muskie. Despite its unusually large size (to British eyes) this lure does have a place in the armoury if you're going to be attacking the big waters. You can fish it around weeded holding areas, and the tandem blades will create resistance which allows you to fish the lure high in the water – but remember to start reeling as soon as the bait hits the water. The trailer treble can be removed, though this may reduce your hooking rate.

Double Buzzer   *PLATE D*

Manufacturer Ryobi, UK

Classification Spinnerbait

Construction Standard spinnerbait layout with tandem Indiana blades, the bottom blade attached by a snap link enabling it to be switched easily. 4/0 hook, good skirt.

Colours/finish Just one colour: Hammered Chrome with Yellow/Black skirt.

Sizes One size: 14g.

Use Widely available in the UK, and a good example of the type. Try switching the bottom blade for a willow blade to create a slightly different sonic pattern – more vibration and less flutter.

Little Joe Spinnerbait   *PLATE D*

Manufacturer   Lindy Little Joe, USA

Classification   Spinnerbait

Construction   Standard format, closed throat, available in single or double Colorado-bladed versions. Sampo swivel, good looking jig head with large painted eye, rubber skirts.

Colours/finish   Six variants: White, Lime/White, Lime/Chartreuse, Chartreuse/Orange, Blue/Chartreuse, Black/Orange.

Sizes   Two sizes: 7g and 11g weight.

Use   A popular and good quality spinnerbait, using top-rated Sampo swivels for free-running blades. Single-blade versions have a spare willow blade, which can be swapped to change the lure into a deeper-running version.

Masterlure Buzzer (aka Barrie's Buzzer)   *PLATE D*

Manufacturer   Ryobi, UK

Classification   Spinnerbait

Construction   Large single Colorado blade, good sized single hook and natural rubber skirt. Fitted with a Sampo swivel. Closed throat so that wire traces will not slip along the arm. Not a true buzzer, this is in fact a spinnerbait.

Colours/finish   Two variants: nickel with black and yellow skirt; copper with brown and orange skirt.

Sizes   Available in 14g size only.

Use   A super surface and sub-surface lure. Barrie's Buzzer – named after Dr Barrie

Rickards, who designed this particular model – is perhaps best known for its *very* large blade which, besides adding to the 'lift' of the lure, gives tremendous rod-shaking vibration as it swims.

Mini-Whacker   *PLATE D*

Manufacturer   Bomber, USA

Classification   Spinnerbait

Construction   Closed-throat spinnerbait, rounded head with large painted eye, single size 1/0 hook, available in single or tandem Colorado-bladed versions. Live rubber skirt.

Colours/finish   Hammered nickel blades, 13 colours, mainly combinations of black, white, chartreuse, lime and yellow. All have red eyes.

Sizes   One size: 55mm long, 4.5g weight.

Use   Despite its small size, this is an effective, well balanced lure, ideal for shallower water where a gentle splashdown is sometimes needed. Use a steady retrieve at a slow-to-medium speed. Very little action on the drop, reasonably strong vibration. Worth trying for pike, perch and trout.

Original Roland Martin   *PLATE D*

Manufacturer   Blue Fox, USA

Classification   Spinnerbait

Construction   Closed-throat spinnerbait with single or tandem Colorado hammered blades. Sampo swivels and a natural rubber skirt give a quality look to this lure, designed by famous Lake Okeechobee-based fishing pro, Roland Martin.

Colours/finish Nine skirt colours available, with gold or silver blades.

Sizes Three sizes: 7g, 11g, 14g

Use As for all spinnerbaits.

Others to try **Roland Martin's Big Bass** (Blue Fox, USA)

Predatory Spinnerbait *PLATE D*

Manufacturer Middy, UK

Classification Spinnerbait

Construction Conventional closed-throat format, Colorado or Willow style blades, small hook (2/0), thinnish skirt.

Colours/finish Available with Silver or Gold blades, skirts in Orange/Black or Chartreuse/White.

Sizes Available in 7g and 11g weight, single or tandem blades.

Use An uninspiring but low-cost spinnerbait, useful for exploring snaggy water. Widely available.

Rattling Spin'R *PLATE D*

Manufacturer Rebel, USA

Classification Spinnerbait

Construction Single Colorado blade, open throat, fish-shaped body, painted eyes, rattling chamber, light filament skirt.

Colours/finish Four colours, all with nickel blade and 'neon' effect: Orange, Chartreuse, Blue and Black Back.

Sizes One size: 10.5g weight.

Use This attractive spinnerbait is designed to give the angler the maximum 'feel' from the lure, and is well suited to those occasions when the fish are biting shy. The Colorado blade gives a nice throb. This spinnerbait casts well and is ideal when fishing small waters with lighter tackle. The open throat should be closed with a small float rubber to avoid the trace sliding up the lure's arms.

Reed Runner *PLATE D*

Manufacturer Northland, USA

Classification Spinnerbait

Construction Twin-bladed spinnerbait with a small Colorado and a large willow-leaf blade on a free-swinging clevis and a full-sized quality swivel. 'Closed throat' attachment eye, neat jig head with interchangeable rubber skirt.

Colours/finish Available in a variety of colour combinations, including Yellow/Orange (Chartreuse Sunrise) and Crawfish (Copper blades with orange/brown skirt).

Sizes Three sizes: 4g, 7g, 11g.

Use A good quality lure, which tends to plane up the water as it is retrieved – it can be used to great effect in shallow water, and is particularly handy for dropping alongside underwater holding areas such as fallen trees. Good for pike and perch.

Spoiler *PLATE D*

Manufacturer Lil' Hustler, USA

Classification Spinnerbait

Construction Double-blade small Colorado with a large willow-leaf blade, closed throat, Sampo swivel and a multicoloured rubber skirt on a painted jig head.

Colours/finish Skirts available in Black, White, Chartreuse/Orange and Chartreuse/ Black; blades come in Gold, Silver and a variety of painted fluorescent colours.

Sizes Available in two sizes: 11g and 7g.

Use A good quality spinnerbait: use as for all others in this class.

CHAPTER ELEVEN
BUZZBAITS

Buzzbaits are a sub-category of the spinners' family. Of similar construction, they have a large propeller, which has two or occasionally three wings, some kind of body, which can be a jig head or (less often) a spoon or a plug type, and almost invariably a skirt or bucktail. Generally, they are in-line spinners, but you can get spinnerbait/buzzbait hybrids with the coathanger-style wire form.

Buzzbaits are the kings of noise and splash, being designed so that the blade operates half in and half out of the water. You need to fish them at a fairly brisk rate of retrieve with the rod tip up to ensure their correct positioning in the water. Choose buzzbaits for shallow, fairly calm water, especially where it's coloured up and fish are forced into hunting by sound rather than sight. Performance can be improved by adding a trailer such as a worm (live or plastic), an extra skirt and/or a trailer hook.

———— ♦ ————

Buzz-Ard Buzzer   *PLATE D*

Manufacturer   Northland, USA

Classification   Buzzer

Construction   Jig head with a rubber skirt, wired to a large aluminium blade. Open throat.

Colours/finish   A range of 12 colours is available, including such exotics as Purple Tequila. Favourites are Chartreuse Sunrise (orange and yellow) and plain Chartreuse. The blade is coloured, as well as the jig head and skirt.

Sizes   Two sizes: 135mm long, 7g weight; 135mm long, 10.5g weight.

Use   Cast out to a suspected fish-holding area and retrieve steadily, holding the rod tip up to create an alluring trail of vibration and bubbles. The sound and sight generated by this bait will trigger pike to strike, especially early in the season, when the fish are particularly active.

Clacker   *PLATE D*

Manufacturer   Lindy Little Joe, USA

Classification   Buzzbait

Construction   Coathanger-type, stainless-steel wire construction with open throat, large jig head with painted eye, good quality rubber skirt and large counter-balanced buzz blade with pierced holes.

Colours/finish   Six colours: White, Lime/White, Lime/Chartreuse, Chartreuse/Orange, Blue/Chartreuse, Black/Orange.

Sizes   Available in one size only: 114mm long, 21g weight.

Use The Clacker makes a distinctive clacking sound as the blade rotates, and the pierced holes in the blade produce a stream of tiny bubbles. This, coupled with the movement of the skirt and the fish-imitating jig head, attracts lurking fish to strike at a possible food source. The Clacker will come up to the surface even when a slow retrieve is used, but you need to keep your rod tip up. Fish this using a steady, slow retrieve, with an occasional burst of speed. Try running it parallel with the bank ahead of you, or over weed lying just under the surface. It should be kept on the surface, since it really doesn't have a lot of effect if you try to fish it at depth.

Goldwing   *PLATE D*

Manufacturer Hildebrandt, USA

Classification Buzzbait

Construction Double-winged propeller blade, single hook, 70-strand vinyl skirt, double-pronged wire weed guard.

Colours/finish Comes in 24k gold- or nickel-plated blade, with 18 skirt colours, including the favourite chartreuse and fluorescent red.

Sizes Two sizes available: 7g and 14g.

Use A high quality lure designed to be fished on the top of, or just below, the water's surface. Buzzbaits in general tend to be most effective on still, calm days, and this is no exception. The propeller stirs up a lot of vibration, and it seems that the noise rather than the appearance of the lure is the main attraction, which makes it a useful option when water is coloured up. The weed guard gives protection from snagging, so try the Goldwing fished across weed beds and lily pads early in the morning or at the end of a day's fishing. Attractive to all predators.

Hawaiian Wiggler   *PLATE C*

Manufacturer Arbogast, USA

Classification Buzzbait

Construction A fishy, head-weighted lure with large single hook, single-bladed prop, and two-pronged weed-guard. A natural rubber tail completes this strange looking lure.

Colours/finish Six colours: Black, Yellow, Shad, Frog, Yellow Coach Dog, Red/White.

Sizes Available in three sizes: 4g, 7g, 11g.

Use Weird though this lure looks, you *can* fish it right through lily beds on and just under the surface. Developed in 1944, the Hawaiian Wiggler (originally called Sputterfuss) was amongst the first commercial buzzbaits to arrive on the market.

Kilty Tri-lure   *PLATE D*

Manufacturer Kilty Lure Co, Ireland

Classification Buzzbait

Construction In-line buzzbait, stainless-steel wire, bullet-shaped brass body incorporating a hand-tied bucktail, treble hook.

Colours/finish Gold, silver or copper blade, plus a range of bucktail colours, including a good red.

Sizes One size: 110mm long.

Use Designed in Ireland with pike and salmon in mind, this long-casting buzzbait is perfect for fishing the big loughs. The long-nosed blade and bucktail create a lot of surface disturbance and a trail of bubbles. Fish along the surface with a steady retrieve.

Oki Twister

PLATE D

Manufacturer   Lil' Hustler, USA

Classification   Buzzbait

Construction   Standard spinnerbait format, supported by two arms with twin contra-rotating buzz blades. Large single hook (as normal), living rubber skirt, closed throat.

Colours/finish   Blades in aluminium only, skirts in black, white, orange and chartreuse and black and chartreuse.

Sizes   One size only: 7g.

Use   The contra-rotating blades set up tremendous surface splashing, which is a very useful summer trick to madden those early-season pike! Work with a steady retrieve, keeping the rod tip up. The hook carries a little lower in the water than for an in-line buzzbait.

Skitter Buzzbait

PLATE D

Manufacturer   Lindy Little Joe, USA

Classification   Buzzbait

Construction   Buzz blade with pierced holes, four orange spacer/attractor beads on shaft, integral Colorado-shaped 'spoon' above a single hook, skirt holder, double-pronged weed guard.

Colours/finish   Two finishes: Silver and Gold.

Sizes   Two sizes: 120mm long, 10.5g weight and a smaller 7g version.

Use   A very weedless surface buzzer, the spoon enables the lure to ride right on the top

of the water. The free-revolving sonic blade is designed to create a stream of tiny bubbles and spray as it moves through the water, the sound and sight of which act as a fish attractor. The skirt holder allows for the secure attachment of a trailer – a rubber skirt, soft worm or light rubber minnow are all possibilities here – which adds to the attraction of the lure. Another early season pike lure, this is also just the kind of lure that will attract a chub.

Sputterbug

PLATE D

Manufacturer   Arbogast, USA

Classification   Buzzbait

Construction   Big-bodied lure with cut-away head, front-mounted prop and vinyl skirt. Two treble hooks, painted eyes.

Colours/finish   Some 14 colour options, ranging from black through a range of mottled coach dog finishes to silver flash and the ever popular red head. The perch pattern is particularly striking.

Sizes   Two sizes: 102mm long, 7g weight; 127mm long, 17.5g weight.

Use   Primarily a surface bait, which will dive a few inches when jerked. Retrieved fast with the rod tip up, the head spinner creates a noisy surface commotion and bow wave. Fished slower, a paddling sound can be achieved, and the lure can even be popped. Very free-turning spinner; the hula skirt adds movement. Often provokes a strike just after landing in the water.

Others to try   **Sputterbuzz** (Arbogast, USA); similar to above, but with a weedless treble.

Thundertoad

PLATE D

Manufacturer   Southern Lure Co, USA

Classification   Buzzbait

Construction   Stainless-steel wire, transparent plastic triple-winged blade, soft, hollow rubber 'toad' body contained by double hook, rubber skirt. Comes with an extra 'stinger' hook.

Colours/finish   A range of 14 colours, including four fluorescents and three spotty ones; skirts are in contrasting colours.

Sizes   One size: 105mm long, 14g weight.

Use   Thundertoad is fished as a standard buzzbait, but it allows you to pause during retrieve, give the lure short twitches, and in fact utilize all the repertoire of surface lure techniques. Very easy to fish – you can fling this one around weed and lily pads and not fear getting caught up. However, you do need to check occasionally to make sure the body of the lure is still nestling safely between the two points of the hook – it's this which makes it weedless. Keep alert when fishing this lure: you do need to set the hook. If fish are coming short, add the stinger hook. This often does the trick (but remember, it makes the lure slightly less weedless).

CHAPTER TWELVE
JIGS AND MISCELLANEOUS LURES

This section covers jigs, artificial worms, plastic fish and other items which don't easily fit in elsewhere.

Plastic fish have been around for a long time in one form or another, but modern materials and manufacturing techniques have brought quality and style to new heights. Today's soft plastic fish are extremely lifelike when rigged for sink and draw, and presumably they must also *feel* more lifelike to a fish. Small ones can be tipped on to a lure for extra attraction. The addition of flavours such as fish oils does seem to enhance their effectiveness in attracting predators.

The Americans have developed the art of jigging with artificial worms (and other artificials) and with this development has come a huge range of wiggly, squishy, rainbow-coloured creatures – fish, mice, frogs, newts, salamanders, slugs, spiders, bees, crayfish, lizards and even snakes! They are frequently supplied impregnated with scents, and their variety is seemingly endless. The jigs which are described in this section, and many thousands more, are normally used in conjunction with these worms, although the worms are often used alone, mounted on a large single hook.

This style of fishing has spread into Europe over the past few years, where pike, perch, chub, zander, trout and largemouth bass are all commonly taken on artificial plastic baits. Here in the UK, however, the style has not yet gained popular acceptance, but the fish are ready . . .

Also included in this section are bass bugs, large flies used by a small number of enthu-siasts for pike, chub and sea fishing – another section of the sport which will surely develop over the coming years.

———— ◆ ————

Bass bugs (Crystal Dragon, Mouse, Frog, Diving Shiner, Beetle) *PLATE O*

Manufacturer Hank Roberts, USA

Classification Coarse flies

Construction In essence, these are oversized flies, mostly tied on 2/0 hooks. Bass bugs use various materials, including bristle, feather, maribou, suede etc, to represent mice, frogs, fry, bees, beetles and other creatures.

Colours/finish Both natural colour representations and brightly coloured variants, weighing no more than a gram or two.

Use These lures can be fished either with a fly rod on conventional fly lines. Alternatively, they're just heavy enough to be cast using a light line – say 6–8lb on a light spinning rod and baitcasting or fixed spool reel. They mainly float, but there are some sinkers. The intention is to attract fish which are feeding towards the surface. Highly recommended as a fun method for chub and perch, but will also fool zander and pike. Trout probably wouldn't say no either!

116

C.C. Spoon

PLATE O

Manufacturer   Cordell, USA

Classification   Jigging spoon

Construction   Long, narrow flat spoon, thick in proportion to its size. Heavy-duty rust-proof treble hook.

Colours/finish   Silver with a dimpled finish and a stamped CC at the head.

Sizes   Two sizes: 51mm long, 10.5g weight; 76mm long, 21g weight.

Use   This dense spoon will cast well, even in windy conditions, and sink quickly to the desired depth even in fast-running water. Use a fast sink-and-draw type retrieve for schooling fish, or jig for suspended fish.

Flying Lure

PLATE O

Manufacturer   Langer Technologies Inc, USA

Classification   Jig

Construction   Lead jig head, fixed single hook, plastic squirt body.

Colours/finish   Grey, Yellow, Purple in a mixed pack – no choice of colour.

Sizes   Four sizes in a mixed pack – no choice of sizes.

Use   This unusual lure has aroused much curiosity. It has the ability to swim backwards, i.e., away from the angler, and can thus reach under structures such as pontoons and overhangs where fish may lurk. Initial experiences with this lure are inconclusive; some people have been disappointed, others

enthusiastic. We are not fully convinced, especially as we haven't had a fish on one yet! At the time of writing, you have to buy a whole pack of these lures (which are only available from one mail order source) to find out if you like them, and you can't get replacements for the squirts, which are very susceptible to damage. We understand that plans are afoot to make the Flying Lure available in smaller packs – one to watch out for.

Jerk Jigger

PLATE O

Manufacturer   Hildebrandt, USA

Classification   Jig

Construction   Metal tube with a solid raked back head. Two trebles, belly hook attached with split ring, additional tail split ring, rubber skirt.

Colours/finish   Four colours: Red/White, Red/Silver, Chartreuse/Silver, Chartreuse/Gold, available with or without vinyl skirts.

Sizes   Five sizes: 21g, 28g, 32g, 42g, 56g.

Use   Extra-strong corrosion-proof construction and heavy Mustad hooks make this an ideal lure for saltwater use. Particularly useful when fishing deep water from a boat or a pier, and designed to attract schooling fish. Match the weight to the depth of water – the deeper the water, the heavier the weight – but also remember that the fish will be looking for something falling quite slowly, not dropping like a stone!

Little Mickey

PLATE O

Manufacturer   Cordell, USA

Classification   Jigging spoon

Construction   A thick (for its size), oval, dimpled slab with a dressed treble.

Colours/finish   Silver, dressed in white with a red thread.

Sizes   One size: 38mm long, 7g weight.

Use   Can be used for fresh or saltwater, suitable for trout in streams and brooks. Use a standard cast and retrieve method – the lure has a nice flutter – or jig it into deep water from a boat.

Soft plastic baits (Top Gun, Big Wag, Grub illustrated)   *PLATE O*

Manufacturer   Riverside, USA (amongst very many firms making similar baits)

Construction   Injection-moulded, soft plastic lures of various shapes and sizes, often impregnated with fish-attracting flavours and salts. Some have hook mounting points built into the moulding. They come without hooks, and you mount them yourself.

Colours/finish   These three examples all come in sizes ranging from 100–175mm and in a wide variety of dazzling colour combinations, often incorporating glitter. Other patterns include crayfish, slugs, twin-tailed worms, lobworms, small fish, eels, leeches, frogs, mice etc.

Use   Soft baits can be used in conjunction with jigs, spinnerbaits, spinner spoons and plugs, or mounted on their own on a special, long shanked offset hook, with or without a jighead. The range available is vast, as this is one of *the* popular bass techniques in the US, in particular in the Southern states. Reasonably cheap to buy, you can use them in any number of ways to enhance existing lures or on their own. The field is wide open for experiment over here, and you can find your own special killing method. Try them for summer chub, perch, zander, small pike, trout, and of course, in the sea.

Supershad   *PLATE O*

Manufacturer   Renosky, USA

Classification   Soft artificial fish

Construction   Soft, very lifelike fish with printed 'fish' finishes. Has entry and exit holes ready for hooking rigs. Fat paddle tail gives balance and action.

Colours/finish   Four natural patterns: Smelt, Perch, Rainbow Trout and (superb) Brown Trout, plus five glitter-impregnated sparkle colours.

Sizes   Eight sizes, from a monster 250mm long, 42g herring-sized bait and including one of 170mm at 28g, and one of 115mm at 14g, down to a microscopic fry-sized 2g version.

Use   A superb soft bait, ideal for sink and draw or wobbling. The simplest rig consists of threading wire trace with a baiting needle through the mouth and out through the vent hole and attaching to the vent end a good sized treble. A second hook can be fixed at the mouth. A very well proven lure, primarily intended for pike. However, smaller sizes are gaining popularity for perch and chub.

Others to try   Proffi-Blinker (GMBH, Germany).

Whistler Jig   *PLATE O*

Manufacturer   Northland, USA

Classification   Spinning jig

Construction   Moulded and painted jig-head, large painted eyes, mounted on a large cranked single hook. The jig features a propeller blade mounted immediately behind the head.

Colours/finish   Six colours: White, Yellow, Fluorescent Chartreuse, Fluorescent Orange, Fluorescent Pink, Fluorescent Green, all with silver propeller blade. A range with 'neon-tone'-painted prop blades is also available.

Sizes   Available in one size only, 50mm long, 10g weight.

Use   This jig is designed for use in conjunction with soft plastic worms, squirt, or small soft plastic fish. Generally fished sink and draw, the jig adds the vibration from the propeller to the seductive waving of the worm tail to great effect. The propeller slows down the jig's descent in the water, giving the fish more chance to take the bait. The Whistler Jig can also be used with a real worm in freshwater or with a rag or lugworm for mullet, bass or inshore pollack.

Wiggle Jig   *PLATE O*

Manufacturer   Gaines Phillips, USA

Classification   Jig

Construction   Shield-shaped lead head, painted eyes, single stainless-steel hook, sparsely dressed.

Colours/finish   Ten simple colour combinations based around black, white, yellow and red.

Sizes   Two sizes: 45mm long (including hook), 7g; 30mm long (including hook), 3.5g.

Use   The head design makes the lure land in a head-down, hook-up presentation. It wobbles delicately on retrieve. Most commonly used for bonefish – thus of interest to anglers heading for sea-fishing exploits in warmer climates – it's also said to be effective for a wide range of fresh and saltwater species. Add a section of cut bait or a worm (plastic or real) for added attraction.

MAIN LURE SUPPLIERS

The Tackle Shop, Bridge Rd, Gainsborough, Lincs; tel. (0427) 613 002. Retail fishing tackle.

Friendly Fisherman, 25 Camden Rd, Tunbridge Wells, Kent, TN1 2PS; tel. (0892) 528 677. Retail fishing tackle, specializing in mail order lures.

The Harris Angling Company, Blacksmith House, Church Rd, East Ruston, Norfolk, NR12 9HL; tel. (0692) 581 208. Specialists in lures and lure fishing tackle (mail order only).

Veals of Bristol, 306 Central Park, Hengrove, Bristol, BS14 9BX; tel. (0275) 892 000. Retail fishing tackle, also mail order.

Charlie Bettell Lures, 96 Bury Fields, Brundall, Norwich, NR13 5QQ. tel. (0603) 714 352. Hand-made lures.

Go Fish, PO Box 153, Coventry, CV3 6ST. Specialists in mail order.

Walkers of Trowell, Nottingham Rd, Trowell, Nottingham, NG9 3PA. Retail fishing tackle, also mail order.

Bass Pro, 1935, S. Campbell, Springfield, MS 65898, USA. American mail order company.

Cabela's, 812, 13th Avenue, Sidney, NE 69160-0001, USA. American mail order company.

SUGGESTED READING

Spinning and Plug Fishing, Rickards and Whitehead (Boydell & Brewer, 1985)
Catching Pike on Lures, Holgate (Cast Publications, 1991)
Fishing with Artificial Lures, Steinberg (Cy DeCosse Inc., 1985)
Northern Pike and Muskie, Steinberg (Cy DeCosse Inc., 1992)
Modern Pike Rigs, Lumb (1993)
Lure Fishing, Ladle & Casey (A & C Black, 1988)
The Ten Greatest Pike Anglers, Rickards and Bannister (Boydell & Brewer, 1991)
The Predator Becomes the Prey, Bailey and Page (The Crowood Press, 1985)
Pike – In Pursuit of Esox Lucius, Page and Bellars (The Crowood Press, 1990)
Spinners Delight, Thurlow Craig (Hutchinson, 1951)
Pike, Gay and Rickards (Boydell & Brewer, 1989)

USEFUL ADDRESSES

Angler's Co-operative Association 23 Castlegate, Grantham, Lincs NG31 6SW.

Bass Angler's Sportfishing Society c/o 37 Miles Ave, Sandford Woods, Wareham, Dorset, BH20 7AS.

Foster An Angler (The anglers' charity) Anchor Cottage, East Tisted, Alton, Hants GU34 3RS; tel. (042) 058 625. This charity for children with special needs gives deprived children a chance to experience the fun of fishing. They welcome donations, help and any old tackle you can spare.

The Lure Anglers' Society of Great Britain 31a Botanic Rd, Southport, Lancs, PR9 7NG.

National Association of Specialist Anglers 27 Ashworth Avenue, Ruddington, Nottingham, NG11 6GD.

National Mullet Club 60 Powerscourt Rd, North End, Portsmouth, PO2 7JG.

Perchfishers 34 Markville Gardens, Caterham, Surrey, CR3 6RJ.

The Pike Anglers Club of Great Britain c/o 24F Red Lodge Rd, Bexley, Kent, DA5 2JW.

The Salmon and Trout Association Fishmongers Hall, London Bridge, London, EC4R 9EL.

Welsh Salmon and Trout Association Swyn Teifi, Pontrhudendigaid, Ystrad Meurig, Dyfed.